# "LET ME KNOW MYSELF . . ."

## Reflections on the Prayer
## of Augustine

*Donald X. Burt, O.S.A.*

THE LITURGICAL PRESS
Collegeville, Minnesota

www.litpress.org

## A Note About the Translations

I can blame no one but myself for the quotations from Augustine. By and large they are my attempt to render the thought of Augustine in modern terms. Thus they are not word-for-word translations from the Latin. I believe they are true to Augustine's meaning. Whether they are successful renditions is for the reader to decide.

Cover design by Ann Blattner. Illustration: Augustine detail from "Altar of the Fathers of the Church," Alte Pinakothek, Munich. By Michael Pacher.

1     2     3     4     5     6     7     8

Library of Congress Cataloging-in-Publication Data

Burt, Donald X.
    "Let me know myself—" : reflections on the prayer of Augustine /
Donald X. Burt.
        p. cm.
    Includes bibliographical references.
    ISBN 0-8146-2800-1 (alk. paper)
        1. Self—Religious aspects—Christianity.  2. Augustine, Saint, Bishop
of Hippo.  3. Spirituality—Catholic Church.  I. Title.

BT713.B87 2002
233—dc21                                                      2001050267

# Contents

## Part 3
## On the Road to Discovery

# Introduction

Seek your own good, my soul. Each one has his own good, and
every creature has some type of good which when attained
completes it and makes it perfect. And so, my soul, seek your
own good which is the highest good, God. There are many
other goods proper to creatures less than human beings. Cattle
seek only to fill up their stomachs, to avoid distress, to sleep, to
wake cheerfully, to be healthy, and to propagate. This is their
good established for them by the Creator of all things. Can you
be satisfied with the good life of cattle? You cannot. You must
raise up your sights to the God who is the good of all goods
(*Commentary on Psalm 102*, 8).

Spirituality is one of those impressive words that is suffi-
ciently vague as to mean anything one wants. In its most broad
sense it can encompass how one sees the world and deals with
it in a worthy human fashion. In this meaning it includes
knowledge of my "self," knowledge of the world outside my
"self," and the development of rules of action for making wise
and prudent decisions about living in the world.

The term can be off-putting. It brings to my mind those
morning meditations based on thoughts someone else created,
conveniently organized into three or four points. In the early
days of my religious life this exercise was done at five-thirty in
the morning, an auspicious time giving sleep to the weak and an
excuse for the strong to avoid further "spiritual thinking"
through the midst of their busy day. In our present busy secular
environment a discussion of spirituality can be sleep-inducing

in lecture form and conversation-inhibiting in small groups. The sentence "Let me now talk about my spirituality" produces drowsiness in audiences and tempts normally patient friends to walk quickly away. Offering a course in spirituality invites the humbling experience of having it canceled for lack of enrollment. I know this from personal experience.

It is unfortunate that this is so, because a developed spiritual life is a strong support for us as we make our wandering way through the sometimes pandemonium of daily life. Most of us can identify with the trials of that poor mythological fellow, Sisyphus, day after day rolling a huge boulder up a steep mountain only to have it roll back down to the bottom to be pushed up again. We seem to be doing something similar day in and day out: rising, off to our chores, four hours of labor, lunch, more labor, finish our tasks, dinner, sleep . . . and then to another day with the same old rock to be rolled up the same boring hill. On most days we go through the process in an unthinking way, but then suddenly we may stop in the midst of our routine and ask, "Why? Is that all there is? Is this blindly mechanical existence the total meaning of my life?" These questions, which force us beyond the pedestrian grind of our daily lives, are the beginning of a movement toward spiritual reflection. It is in this realm of the spirit, the vision of human life that goes beyond the humdrum of everyday life and material needs, that we begin our efforts to make sense of our ordinary day-by-day existence.

The broad picture of each of our lives is much the same. At birth we are dropped into time. At burial we are lowered into eternity. In the meantime we make our mark on history, singing our own particular note in the song of the universe. Each person intones a different note, but each is faced with the same challenge: to live this life in such a way that it can become part of the eternal song chanted by God through his creatures.

To live and die is a lonely task. No one can live our lives except ourselves; no one can die our death. And no one can take the consequences of the way we have lived and died except ourselves. Our main concern must then be to live so as not to die forever—to avoid suffering that terrible death of separation from God, that *second* death that Augustine rightly considered more terrifying than that first death, which ends our time in time. Our most important duty in this life must be to take care of ourselves, to see to our own eternal happiness, our own salvation. To be sure, we must love others as ourselves, but we must love ourselves first.

St. Augustine was well aware of this truth. He was convinced that no venture was more important than reflection on his own destiny. Describing the nature of the universe (speculative philosophy) or examining human societies (practical philosophy) were noble tasks, but they must always give way to the study of the path of one's own perfection. At the same time, Augustine's primary concern about his own destiny did not mean that he was a rugged individualist, a self-centered egoist caring nothing about the world beyond himself. His own salvation, his own happiness, was indeed his chief goal in life, and he knew this goal could not be achieved without concern for others. But it would clearly have been absurd to work at saving others while sacrificing his own spiritual health. To paraphrase Scripture: "What good is it to save the whole world and lose your own soul?"

In the passage that begins this reflection, Augustine speaks about the different goods of the different orders of creation (humans versus cattle, and so forth), but his command to his soul, "Seek your *own* good," is a command addressed to every human being. Though all of us share a common need to be united to God in order to be happy and perfected as humans, each of us achieves that goal in our own special way. Each human has been created by God to fulfill a specific and individual purpose. Each reflects in their own special way the image of God. Each one is guided toward salvation down a path especially fitted to their needs by the God who dwells within. The most important task for each of us is to discover that path, accept it, and follow it bravely till it reaches its end: the heavenly city where God dwells.

After years of living a pagan lifestyle and searching for the meaning of life in various ideologies (Manicheanism, Neoplatonism, skepticism), Augustine finally came to the Christian point of view. Thereafter the spiritual life of a human being meant one thing for him: the attempt to arrive at union with that person who was all-good: the infinite, immutable God. But where in this life is that God to be found? God's primary place (if that is a proper word) is in that immense realm beyond time, an area far removed from human experience and impossible to reach as long as we continue our pilgrimage on earth. The very fact that we are pilgrims is a sign we have not yet arrived at our destiny. Where then are we to find God in this world?

Augustine's answer is that we must look within. God is everywhere, but in creation his strongest presence is in each individual human being. The beginning of the search for God must thus begin with the discovery of self. It is for this reason that Augustine prayed, "O unchanging God, let me know myself; let me know you. That is my prayer" (*Soliloquies*, 2.1.1).

The purpose of the essays that follow is to offer some reflections on the first part of this prayer—the discovery of self. Perhaps in honestly facing ourselves we will have taken the first step toward discovery of God.

# Part 1

## *Setting the Scene*

Consider the fact that God created human beings upright and healthy. Just think of the sweet happiness of that first couple bound together in love in paradise. Although it was so brief that none of their children experienced it, and even though we learn about it in this harsh environment of our present life, which sometimes seems like an everlasting trial despite all our efforts to make progress, even so, when you come to think about it, we are unable to describe adequately these first great gifts bestowed on the human race by the goodness of God (*City of God*, 22.22).

Before getting in too deep in the search for my self, it is advisable to examine the environment in which my search takes place. Like Augustine, I can turn to Scripture to discover some explanation of my present condition. Like Augustine, when I turn to my self, there are some facts so blatant they need no discovery. They force themselves upon me whether I will it or not. Thus I know that I am a divided self torn by conflicting desires. I am a mystery hard to comprehend. And, most humbling of all, I know that I am "cracked" and not as perfect as I pretend to be. My first problem will then be to be honest with my self. In this section the reflections are aimed at these issues, issues that set the scene for any further investigation.

# The Mystery of My Self

> O Lord, you alone know what I am. Even though Paul said, "No man knows what he is in himself except his own spirit" (1 Cor 2:1), there is much about me that even my spirit does not know. With regard to these unknowns, my ignorance will last until that day when "darkness shall be made as the noonday in your sight" (Isa 58:10) (*Confessions*, 10.5.7).

Augustine's prayer "Let me know myself!" is a hard task to accomplish. There is a darkness inside each of us that is difficult to penetrate. Our present is often cloudy and our future is beyond prediction. As Augustine admitted to his friends, "I may be able to know to some extent what I am today, but what I shall be tomorrow I do not know" (*Sermon 179*, 10).

Augustine seemed to become more aware of this interior darkness as he grew older. It is not surprising. When Augustine was young he, like most of the rest of us, was more interested in externals, things like doing well in school, being appreciated by others, satisfying sexual desire, becoming a success in a noble profession that paid well. Questions about the nature of the universes outside and inside himself were solved by assuming that his days were under the control of forces beyond his power to change. He thought to himself, "There is no use worrying about the future when nothing can be done to change it. There is no use agonizing over the past if I was not responsible for it."

In some ways this attitude of the young Augustine was like those who today blame all events on fate or the power of the stars and get on with their lives singing, "Why worry? Be happy!"

Only when we get older (and sometimes not even then) do we begin to look inside ourselves to discover what has become of us, what we have *really* done with those precious moments of time that have been granted to us. Perhaps we don't think about writing a book of confessions until we are older because in our youth we do not think we have that much to confess. When we are young there are no missed opportunities, only opportunities that are still to come. When we are young we are more unformed than deformed.

When Augustine wrote his own *Confessions* at forty, there was much to consider—where he had gone wrong and the mystery of how his life was finally made right. At forty the memories were still fresh, and the energy to write them down was still strong. As a middle-aged man he was ready for some serious writing. The only book he wrote in his youth was a somewhat pompous, abstract (and unpublished) volume on beauty in general. It took some "growing up" before he began to look inward and even more growing before he was able to perceive the beauty shining through the darkness in his "self."

Such ventures into self-discovery can be frightening. Those who look deeply into their true selves are like hardy spelunkers who plunge deep into the crevasses and caverns of the earth's crust, sometimes trapped in crevices too narrow for exploration, sometimes lost in the silent, shadowed passages of that world beneath the surface of pleasant ordinary experience. To plunge inside ourselves can be just as terrifying because there is no science to guide our way, there is no comforting light to carry with us except that dim lamp of reason, which operates none too well even in daylight. Indeed, as Augustine discovered, the only true illumination that can be found in the cavern of the self is a light shining within whose source is as mysterious as the self it tries to reveal.

Once I begin that journey inside myself, I soon learn the truth of Augustine's descriptions of his own experience. I find an abyss deeper than any sea (*Commentary on Psalm 41*, 14; *Commentary on Psalm 76*, 18). I discover that the hidden life throbbing inside the depths of my spirit is a site with many facets and many passages marvelous beyond my wildest dreams (*Confessions*, 10.17.26).

Perhaps this shadowy area is first revealed in my dreams. Now that I am older I find my sleep is fitful with frequent "risings." At night my mind becomes like a multiplex theater where every interval of sleep has a different dream, strange stories thankfully only half-remembered in the day. Mostly the dreams are not pleasant. They present recurrent scenes of embarrassment, fear, and uncontrolled passion. I have come to believe that such dreams are flowing from the darkness deep within myself, a darkness I am reluctant to admit in the course of the day. It is as though God is saying to me, "This too is part of you. You are not as perfect as you sometimes pretend to be. There was no folly, cowardice, perversity, fallacy, or fetish beyond possibility for you if my grace had not acted to protect you from yourself."

Such self-discovery can be humbling, and it is always difficult and exhausting because to reveal myself to myself I must first overcome myself. It is not a battle easily won. Beginning this journey into the depths of myself, I quickly come to understand Augustine's words that it is easier to record the "comings and goings" of the hairs on my head than to keep track of the surging feelings coursing through my heart day after day (*Confessions*, 4.14.22). I discover with him that this work of exploring that which is the closest thing to me, my very self, is a chore analogous to the punishment imposed on Adam. Like the fallen Adam I find that to support my life I must dig into a field difficult to cultivate. In my search for my "self" my life becomes a task of "too much sweat" (Gen 3:17-19) (*Confessions*, 10.16.25).

Despite the difficulty, my search for self must be done. If I cannot live with the truth about myself, I can never hope to discover the truth about God. Unless I am able to find the true "me," I will have nothing of value to offer others for them to love. Without some honest discovery of my self, there will be no "me" to be loved. I will be an empty shell of no importance.

# The Inner and Outer Self

The inner self and the outer self are not the same. When we speak of the "outer self," we mean the body. The "inner self" refers to a person's soul. They are different but together they form one person (*Letter 238*, 12).

**O**ne of the reasons why my self is so mysterious, so difficult to discover, is that it has two aspects. One of these is what Augustine calls the "outer man" (or "outer self"), that external "me" that the world sees, the "me" that can be measured and weighed and shaped by empirical science. It is my body, that fleshly shell in which and through which I live my life in this material world. Even though no one can completely understand its workings, it is at least somewhat evident to the external world. Its illnesses can be treated with medicines; its corrupted parts can be cut away through surgery. It can be shaped by exercise and diet in an attempt (often a vain attempt) to produce that "perfect body" so glorified by society.

The second part of my self, my inner self, is not so easily molded or perfected. Only God sees it perfectly. I can perceive it sometimes and then only imperfectly. Others come to know it indirectly, either by inference from the way I act or by my own testimony about myself, a testimony that is always incomplete and sometimes inaccurate. This inner self is the seat of my knowledge, choice, and action. It is the center of energy for all that my body does; it is the force that holds it together. If my inner self should ever leave, my outer self would quickly fall apart.

The discovery of our inner self is a difficult task that lasts a lifetime. We have no consciousness of it at birth, and it takes hard work and the help of God to become aware of it at all. This is so because the process of discovery demands moral development more than development of the intellect. Although some grasp of the truth is necessary, it is more important to refine one's life than to hone one's mind. Unfortunately some never complete the task. Remaining infantile, they never get beyond grasping for those external goods that promise to make them comfortable. They live a life on the surface of reality and become nothing more than empty shells with pleasing exteriors.

It is unfortunate when this happens because the inner self is the center of and most important part of me. It is the foundation of my special value, that part of myself that justifies my claim to be better than the rest of creation. As Augustine observed, "If you only take into account the outer self, the only difference between human beings and beasts is that humans stand upright" (*The Trinity*, 12.1).

However, as glorious as it may be, this inner self is not the complete human being. Unlike those who maintained that the human being *is* the rational soul now unfortunately trapped in the gross flesh of the body, Augustine insisted that the human is a being composed of *both* soul and body (*City of God*, 13.24.2; *The Trinity*, 7.4.7; 15.7.11). Thus my complete self is not like the vibrant growing center of a maturing egg temporarily confined in a hard shell destined some day to break and set me free. Rather, my self is more like the planet earth, a raging fire momentarily confined by a thin solid crust, periodically exploding in volcanic eruptions of wise insight and heroic choices completely unexpected by those who can see only the shell. Just as the surface of the earth is as much "earth" as the fire within, so too my body is as much "me" as that mysterious shimmering spirit that supports it and gives it warmth. If the surface of the earth should disappear, the earth itself would perish. So too with me. When my body fails, my immortal soul may continue, but it is my *soul*; it is not *me*. I (the complete "me") exist after death only as a possibility waiting in the mind and plan of God until re-formed again through resurrection of my body and its reunion with my soul.

Frankly, it would be sometimes easier if I were only my soul, my inner self. There would be some comfort in not being identified with this craggy old body, which is the source of so much discomfort, inconvenience, and embarrassment to my glorious spirit. Without the body I would not need to take care that I not drink too much coffee before beginning a long speech. Without the body I would not be tempted to spend so much time preening and readjusting parts of my outer self that I forget the needs of my inner self, that self that often requires reconstructive surgery more than cosmetics. I would not need to heed Augustine's warning that "the more attention we pay to the ornaments and finery of the outer self, the less attention we pay to our inner self" (*Sermon 161*, 11).

Without my body my passion for the lovely people I love would not be tarnished by the sometimes ignoble desires of my carnality. Without a body I would no longer fear cancer and those innumerable afflictions that can painfully tear it apart. Without the body I would not need to be concerned about my ponderous weight, only about having ponderous thoughts and making weighty decisions.

But all of this is non-corporeal dreaming, and like all dreams it stands in the way of reality. My search for my self must begin by putting aside all fantasies about what might be and facing the reality of what is. And the first part of that reality is that there are two aspects to my life, my material body and my spiritual soul. Together they make me to be ME, and to ignore either part would yield only an incomplete answer to Augustine's prayer, "Let me know myself." By nature I am a "dusty angel," both earthy and ethereal, and as my spirit pulls me toward the heavens and thirsts for eternity, my body is drawn toward earth and decays with the passing of time.

Of course, my body (my outer self) cannot be blamed for all the bad that I do in this life. After all, it has no mind of its own; my outer self does not desire or choose. It is my spirit (my inner self) that does such things, and all of the conflicting desires that sometimes tear me apart have their home in that spirit. My desires for food, drink, and physical pleasure may have roots in my body, but it is my spirit that chooses them. Moreover, my spirit too has its own unique thirsts, incorporeal thirsts that reach even beyond time. As Augustine declares:

> There is an inner thirst and an inner belly because there is an inner self. Even those who live lives dedicated to bodily satisfaction still desire "to live," and this desire for life is a desire of the inner self (*Commentary on the Gospel of John*, 32.2.2–3).

Certainly the vice of pride has little to do with the body. It is a desire for a spiritual good, a desire to be infinitely superior in time and eternity.

But as good as it tries to be, the inner self is persistently distracted by the demands of the outer self, demands for good food, good wine, physical comfort, and sexual satisfaction. Even in matters purely intellectual it can be enticed to concentrate on matters of here and now—the pursuit of earthly success, the pursuit of science rather than wisdom.

None of the physical goods demanded by our outer self are harmful in themselves, but they become destructive when they consume all of our energy. The astronomers Augustine speaks about in the *Confessions* (5.3.4) who could predict the eclipse of the sun but could not see their own eventual eclipse were not bad men, but their attention was terribly misdirected. Similarly, Augustine did not mean to condemn those married people who had sex with their spouses because they enjoyed it. What he did warn against was letting one's physical passion for the loved one stand in the way of friendship, that oneness of heart that is the mark of true love for one's soul mate.

In an ideal world this tension would be under control. I would not live by fits and starts, now reaching for the stars, now plummeting to the depths. To use Augustine's apt phrase, "I would be friends with my body" (*Sermon 155*, 14.15). But this world is not ideal, and as a result our lives become tangled bundles of knots. As we race from the heights to the depths and back again we are tempted to cry out with Augustine: "Who can untie such a tortured and complicated knot?" (*Confessions*, 2.10.18).

An understanding of these complexities of my life, my "twists and turns," may come from knowing something of my history. How did I get where I am with this two-sided self that sometimes is indeed more an aggravation than a joy? To be sure, my ancestors cannot be blamed (or credited) with all that is happening to me now. Many of my problems come from my own action or inaction. I cannot blame my forebears for my being a drunk or a lecher or a fool. But at the same time it does seem that I have come into existence with slightly defective equipment, flaws that now somehow make it easier to become a jackass than an angel. The story of its beginnings may shed some light on the human situation now. It is this story that must be considered next.

# Adam's Loss of Self

> Genesis (2:5-6) gives a description of the human condition before the first sin was committed. In paradise God spoke directly to them through the depths of their inner self. They had no need for words from outside; they were nourished by the waters of that internal spring, that is, by the Divine Truth that flowed deep inside their very "self." Once humans fled from themselves through pride, they ceased to be watered by that inner spring. Through their pride they abandoned their inner self, trying to appear to the world to be something they were not (*On Genesis Against the Manichees,* 2.4.5).

The story told in the book of Genesis describes the original condition of human beings before there was sin. It was a time when God was immediately present to them. He spoke to each human in the silence of their unsullied inner self, and they were illuminated and filled with joy (*A Literal Commentary on Genesis,* 8.12.25). Augustine describes this union as follows:

> The union between humans and God in Eden was like air filled with light. Air does not possess its own luminosity when light is present. Air has not been given its own luminosity, but it becomes lustrous. In much the same way, human beings are filled with light when God is present to them; if God is absent, darkness falls on them. Such separation is not caused by distance in space but by a turning away of the human will (*A Literal Commentary on Genesis,* 8.12.26).

The enlightenment of those guiltless humans was caused not so much by God being *with* them as by God being *in* them. God lived in the very deepest part of their inner selves.

This idyllic existence of humans walking in a garden joined not simply hand in hand but heart to heart with God was not to last. By their sin they fled from their true selves, and in doing so they fled from God. In Gen 3:5 there is recorded the first and always the most dangerous temptation for any human: the temptation to pretend to be a god. It was also the most destructive temptation for them because in order to pretend to be a god they had to lose sight of themselves—their true nature as imperfect, limited, contingent human beings.

It must have been an attractive temptation for those innocent humans. They had everything except one thing: they were not God. It seems very clear that the desire for divine Wisdom was the real passion that drove Eve (Gen 3:6). Many trees could have satisfied her physical hunger, but only the fruit of the forbidden tree carried the satanic promise that, eating it, she could be more than she was.

Eve took the fruit to Adam and together they sinned. Driven by pride, they sought to escape God's rules and become like gods themselves. It is difficult to understand why they wanted this. Where did they get this taste for being gods? They were born (as we are) with an infinite thirst for knowledge and an infinite hunger to possess the "all" that is God. Perhaps this thirsting for everything led them to believe that they could *be* everything. But the only way in which they could try to become infinite gods themselves was to flee from the God who was so powerfully present in their inner selves, and the only way they could do that was to flee from their own true selves.

The disastrous mistake of those first humans soon became apparent in its effects. Immediately after their disobedience "the eyes of both of them were opened and they realized that they were naked" (Gen 3:7). Seeking to be gods by fleeing from their true selves, they discovered not wisdom but shame. They had always been naked, perfectly open in body and soul, but now, after sin, they had something to hide. The concealing of their bodies' intimate parts was symbolic of their suddenly discovered need to hide the emptiness of their inner selves.

It is not surprising that when "they heard the sound of the Lord God moving about the garden" (Gen 3:9) those poor "make-believe gods" tried to hide. The confusion of their minds caused by their sin had its first dramatic manifestation. Since it had been so easy to deny God, they now thought there was a place where they could hide from his sight. But of course God knew exactly where they were, both physically and spiritually. God knew where they stood and what the state of their souls was. That God seemed to speak to them from some distant place in the garden reveals the extent of their separation from him. The word of God had now to be spoken from some place outside themselves.

Those first humans had gone out of themselves trying to be something they were not and had thereby lost the awareness of the presence of God. God's question to them, "Where are you?" was to be a question to God asked by countless generations of humans thereafter. It is the pathetic cry of the lost human, one who has lost the way because of loss of self. It is no wonder those first humans were tormented. When I pretend to be something greater or less than I truly am, I can give no accurate answer to the question "Who am I?" Trying to live a life (be it divine or beastly) that is not mine, it is only natural that I should lose my bearings. Wandering in a now-unfamiliar world, I call out "Where am I?" Those first humans, hearing the question "Where are you?" from the lips of God, could only answer, "We are in a place remote from you. And when we heard you lumbering about so far away, we were afraid" (Gen 3:10). It was a sad moment in human history. For the first time humans were afraid of God. Fleeing from themselves by seeking to be something they could never be, they had lost God.

They also inflicted wounds on their love for each other. They had been created as friends, but their flight from self and God caused cracks to appear in their friendship. Augustine suggests that one of the reasons Adam joined Eve in eating the forbidden fruit of the tree of knowledge was because of a misdirected love for her, a love that prevailed over the obedience he owed God. He did not want her to "go out on a limb" by herself. Perhaps there was also a bit of envy in his decision. If indeed eating the forbidden fruit would give godlike wisdom, Adam was perhaps reluctant to have Eve be the only god in town.

Whatever the motivation that drove Adam and Eve to disobey God, once the deed was done everything changed. Humans began to justify their mistakes by blaming others. Adam blamed Eve and Eve blamed the serpent. In response to God's question "Why did you do it?" Adam whined: "The woman whom you put here with me gave it to me!" (Gen 3:12). In response to the same question, Eve cried: "The serpent tricked me into it, so I ate it" (Gen 3:13). For the first time in the history of creation the lame excuse was heard from human lips: "It is not my fault; the devil made me do it!"

Adam and Eve's unpersuasive attempts at justifying their actions demonstrate that one effect of hiding self from self is the denial of responsibility for one's actions. It also shows what can happen to friendship and love when one has lost oneself. Adam's soul mate had now become the antagonist who had led him to do his dastardly deed. It is hard to imagine a more destructive attack on love than to say of a loved one, "She is the cause of my sin."

Eve at least did not do that. But she certainly did diminish her standing in the universe. She began as a friend of God and then began dreaming of *equaling* God in wisdom. She ended by blaming her actions on a shifty serpent. Her mournful cry "He tricked me!" suggests that despite all the gifts of knowledge and wisdom given freely to her by God, she still tried to pretend that she was a simple soul not adept in the ways of the world and that somehow or other she was being treated unfairly in being blamed for her decision. Her pride was shown in her implied claim that she was so virtuous that any breaking of law could only be due to some malevolent force beyond her control.

It is indeed paradoxical that the first misuse of human freedom seems to have led to its denial.

Those first humans wanted to be on their own. They wanted to be free, but by fleeing from the God who lived deep inside themselves they entered a prison built by their pride. They became trapped in their passion for goods beyond themselves. There was no room for anyone who did not serve their needs. In their flight from themselves they had lost the power to reach out to others in unselfish love.

No longer could they hear clearly the inspirations of the divine Teacher, who in paradise had revealed in the depths of their self truths about themselves and the world. From now on they would have to depend on outside forces, the grace bestowed from outside by God to strengthen them and the law revealed through prophets and Scripture to guide them. Once nourished by an internal spring, now they had to depend on "rain from outside" to make their lives fruitful.

As a result of their loss of self, we now must work out our salvation, not as *innocents* running joyously in paradise hand in hand with God but as wounded solitary pilgrims limping along a rocky path leading to God. Worst of all, to find that path we must now first search for and bravely face our true selves.

## The Old Man and New Man

Those who, like the fallen Adam, bear the image of the earthly man are called "the old man." Those who now bear the image of the heavenly man (Jesus) are called the "new man." The old man is far removed from God; the new man stands before God and is visited and illumined by the light of the divine presence *(Commentary on Psalm 8, 10).*

The understanding of my self comes partially from self-analysis and partially from history. Through analysis of the present condition of my self I can discover (though imperfectly) the ebb and flow of the emotions, convictions, desires, and hopes coursing through me at any moment. Through history I can come to understand the reason for these currents that seem to sweep unbidden through my self. I can perceive that within me there is not only the tension between my inner and outer selves; there is also a continuing, sometimes painful conflict between the forces of what Augustine called the "old man" and "new man."

In paradise the first humans were truly "new." In the first blush of their creation they had the shiny brilliance of all things new. More perfectly than ever after in time, human beings were truly living in the age of the new man; they were the best created reflections of the infinite perfections of God. All this ended with their sin. In their flight from self they were separated from the life-giving presence of God. By departing from God humans became "old" *(Commentary on Psalm 39, 4).*

The old man was the continuing condition of the humans who lived in the period after Adam's sin and before Christ's redemptive death. They were people condemned to live on earth in a crippled condition. After death they were destined to become permanent members of the earthly city, the city built to house Satan. The old man, which was unredeemed humanity, was a people incapable of ever reaching the bliss of heaven. The door was closed, and they had no effective way of gaining entrance. Only after the redemptive act of Christ was it possible for the new man to emerge, humans so bathed in grace they were able to make Christ's sacrifice effective in accomplishing their own personal salvation.

The history of those worldly human beings in whom the old man dominates is quite different from those who have begun to change themselves (with the help of God's grace) into spiritual beings in whom the new man has begun to be formed. Augustine identifies five periods in the life of the "natural" man.

Whether "old" or "new," all humans spend their *infancy* mostly in nourishment and growth. The mind is present, but its activity is limited to recognizing and seeking food and drink and comfort. The experiences of this stage of life are so primitive they are not even retained in memory. This changes as the person progresses through *childhood*. Gradually the mind awakens and gains memory of day-by-day experiences. When the human grows into *adolescence,* physical powers reach their peak, and propagation and parenthood are possible. After adolescence comes the vigor of *maturity,* when the person is now expected to take on public duties and be more observant of law. The wrongdoing that may have been excused with a reprimand in childhood now is liable to penalty since it has become willful disobedience to recognized obligations. Finally, after years of flourishing activity *old age* begins, a somewhat somber period of dullness of mind, weakness of body, greater susceptibility to disease, and an irrevocable drift toward death. For a person who remains in the realm of the old man this is the complete story of their life. As Augustine writes,

This is the life of human beings so long as they have bodily life and are bound only by desire for temporal goods. This is the "old man," the earthy person who lives only for externals (*On True Religion*, 26.48).

The history of the spiritual person, the one who seeks to escape the old man and be renewed into the new man, goes beyond such simple earthy existence. Its phases are not measured by the stages in our physical life but rather in the steps toward our spiritual development. Because of inherited sin and the weakness of infancy, even those destined to achieve the goal of becoming a new man are born as down-to-earth beings concerned only with survival (*On True Religion*, 27.50). Even soon-to-be virtuous humans begin as newborns in whom the spirit has not yet awakened to the possibility of a higher form of life. But as they grow under the influence of grace they begin to be reborn inwardly into the form of the new man.

In the *first* stage of development they are nourished by the examples of good people past and present. In the *second* stage they begin to become more interested in eternal realities than in temporal affairs, moving from respect for secular laws to an understanding of the unchangeable law at the root of the universe. From this they move to a *third* stage, where carnal appetites are united and controlled by reason. Body and spirit become one and the pleasure in sinning is taken away. In the *fourth* stage they move to action, developing the fortitude that enables them to be ready to endure and conquer persecution and the turbulent events of life. In the *fifth* stage they achieve the peace and tranquillity that comes with entering the realm of supreme unchanging Wisdom. In the *sixth* stage they are completely transformed, disinterested in all things temporal, living a life more of eternity than of time, becoming the most perfect image of God they can be in this life. Finally, having lived the life of the new man before death, after death they achieve the *seventh* and ultimate stage of human perfection, a stage in which they enjoy eternal rest and perpetual happiness in union with God (*On True Religion*, 26.49; 27.50).

This image of the old man becoming new Augustine learned from his reading of the Old and New Testaments. Finally coming to appreciate the truth of the Scriptures, he was able to understand why his life was in such turmoil. The story told there took the place of the myth that he had believed when he was a Manichean. It told him that the battle in himself was not between two gods but rather was between two aspects of himself, the old man defending its ground and the new man seeking to conquer new territory. Neither force was overpowering since, although he was strengthened by grace, he (like every human) was still "cracked." It was therefore not surprising to him that the history of every person (apart from Mary the mother of Jesus) was a history of victories and defeats (*Commentary on Psalm 131,* 1).

Augustine's baptism did not cast aside the old man forever. Bad habits die slowly, if at all. Even in the days before his conversion when his new man was striving to break free, it found itself still held back by the habits of the old man. He describes the inner turmoil of those days quite eloquently:

> I longed for the chance to devote myself wholly to you (God) but I was held back, bound not with the iron chains of some foreign abductor but by the bonds of my own iron will. My evil habits held my will. They were like links hanging one on another (which is why I have called it a chain) and their firm bondage held me bound hand and foot. My two wills, one old and one new, one carnal, one spiritual, were in conflict, and their conflict wasted my spirit (*Confessions,* 8.5.10 and 12).

Augustine's experience is shared in some degree by all of us. Despite all our good intentions and our resolve to let the new man take control of our lives, there remains a desire for carnal and temporal goods (*83 Diverse Questions,* 36.2). Constant renewal is necessary because the effects of the old man still lurk within. Even a long life lived virtuously will not necessarily take away aberrant desire. Augustine himself remained forever "in love with love," and though in his later years he never repeated the sexual escapades of his youth, he was still bothered in his middle age by memories of what had been and temptations of what yet could be again (*Confessions,* 10.32.42).

Although we can sense the disturbance of conflicting desires, the ignorance with which we sometimes begin important ventures, and the overwhelming emotion that sometimes clouds our minds and drives us to irrational action, it takes the testimony of faith to tell us why this is so. Just as a skilled doctor will identify the fracture that causes us pain, so the history of humanity as described in Scripture testifies to a crucial truth about ourselves. We have been put into the furnace and have emerged "cracked" (*Commentary on Psalm 99,* 11). We are "cracked pots" sometimes unable to see clearly what we should do, sometimes unable on our own to stir up the moral resolve to do what should be done.

The first step in our renewal must then be to recognize that we need renovation, but this awareness does not always come easily. Commenting on the gospel story of the rich man who tore down his old barn to build new, bigger ones (Luke 12:16-20), Augustine noted that we are often shrewd about such earthly affairs but completely stupid about the state of our soul. We apply proper preventative maintenance on things we own but are foolish when it comes to repairing our own lives (*Sermon 359,* 3). Only when the need for spiritual renewal is recognized can the actual process begin: a process that has its foundation in faith, receives its vigor from contrition for the past, and patiently builds for the future through the development of good habits (*The Trinity,* 4.3.5; *Commentary on Psalm 8,* 10).

Augustine maintained that this life is not a time for being perfect but a time for daily repentance and trying again. He was convinced that God does not expect us to be perfect just now. God only expects us to be sorry and not to despair when suddenly that old man appears in the midst of our celebration at being the new man we assume we already are.

# The Cracked Self

Responding to some of his confreres who came to him with a plan for creating an ideal community composed only of those who were perfect, Augustine asked:

> How will you eliminate those who are not perfect? Those who join you do not even know themselves too well; how in the world can you know them? Many people promise themselves they will live a holy life, but they fail because they have been put into the furnace and have come out cracked (*Commentary on Psalm 99*, 11).

The pursuit of eternal happiness is for every person a story of frequent starts and stops. With the exception of Mary the mother of Jesus, every human life is the tale of twisting and turning down the road to heaven. We do not make our way through life like an arrow plummeting straight and true toward the goal. We are more like tops, spinning perilously down the path, lurching now to one side and now to the other, sometimes falling off as we lose momentum, needing to be picked up and gently nudged toward our destiny. It is not an easy journey for any of us, because (as Augustine points out) there are at least three (and possibly four) challenges that we must face on our way to heaven.

The *first* challenge is to acquire the energy and the wisdom to discover what we must do to gain salvation. Many of us just seem to float through life lulled by the pleasures of daily living. If we think about death at all, we do not worry about when it will happen to us. Only by the grace of God (sometimes veiled in a traumatic experience) can we be impelled to ask serious questions about the direction of our lives (*Commentary on Psalm 106*, 4).

If we do finally develop a taste for the truth and even discover what should be done to reach eternal happiness, we must face the *second* challenge: the need to now *do* what we know should be done. Before we were hungering for some truth, wandering about seeking where we should go. But when we do finally find out what we should do, we discover that we are incapable of making the decision to do it! It is almost as if we are imprisoned by a lifetime of habits that bind us to the place where we are (*Commentary on Psalm 106*, 5).

After we have developed the habit of leading a virtuous life, a *third* difficulty may arise: we may get bored. The monotony of being good day after day may lead to a deep-rooted tedium. Our life may be truly noble, but the fire has gone out. There is no fervor. We have become wholly weary of being holy. Having come so far and having fought so many battles, we become bored with living days of "same old, same old." We become anesthetized by ennui (*Commentary on Psalm 106*, 6).

When we have achieved a continuing fervent, well-ordered life, some of us will be faced with a *fourth* challenge. We may think all our problems are over. We know where we are going. We consistently choose to do the right thing, and we are still enthusiastic despite the virtuous sameness of our lives. Everything is going well with us. No longer are we plagued with the confusion and weakness of will that characterized our life before. But then it happens. Someone (perhaps God) will say, "These folks seem well tied together. Let's put them in charge of others!"

Finally achieving peace within ourselves, we now spend our days worrying about somebody else. Thus, good parents are harried by their wild kids, balanced counselors worry about their unbalanced clients, and saints called to minister to others must take upon themselves the burdens of their unsanctified charges. Augustine himself faced this burden. One day he sighed to his charges: "I must worry that you do not wander. I must worry that you are not trapped by your bad habits. I must worry that you do not lose a taste for the things of God. This bag of troubles that comes from being in charge now presses upon me very much" (*Commentary on Psalm 106*, 7).

As we have seen, such problems in finding and holding onto God were not part of humanity's original condition. In Eden the first human beings were as naturally perfect as they could be and had the potentiality of becoming even more perfect as they solidified their union with the God who was with them and in them. Through a gift that truly could not have been anticipated, they were even made adopted children of God (*Against Faustus the Manichean*, 3.3). They had minds that were clear and were able to avoid error easily. There was a friendly subordination of their senses to their will such that they could effortlessly make good choices, choices that would further their destiny of being united with God for all eternity. Put simply, they could distinguish truth from falsity, good from bad, and they were able to choose wisely (*Incomplete Work Against Julian*, 5.1).

Those innocent human beings had the great gift of "being able not to sin" *(posse non peccare)* if they so chose (*Admonition and Grace*, 12.33). Unfortunately, they did not so choose. They attempted to become like gods, and this pride-filled choice ended their idyllic existence. All that had been above and beyond nature (freedom from death, adoption as children of God) ended, and nature itself became "cracked."

These cracks exhibited themselves primarily as defects in the human intellect and will. Augustine uses the terms *ignorantia* and *difficultas* to designate them and describes them thus:

> What at the present moment are the evils of humanity? Error and weakness. Either you don't know what you should do or, if you do know, you discover that you are too weak to do it. Such confusion and weakness is the root of every evil thing that humans do (*Sermon 182*, 6).

The effects of these disabilities in mind and will have been demonstrated over and over again throughout human history.

In the innocent time before sin the human mind had been limited but reasonably clear. Through that primordial crack of original sin it became clouded. After original sin the human will, which before could rush happily toward true goods presented by intellect, was now not so easily influenced. Perversity took on its own fascination. Human beings began to embrace evil for its own sake. The innocence of Eden was over. The human race had become ornery. Humans said to Evil: "Be THOU my good!"

In Eden humans did good because it was easy; after Eden humans sometimes do evil because it is fun. They pretend they are bound by no limitations. They act as though they know everything there is to know. Sadly, their condition is just the opposite. Now they cannot even do the good they want to do. Where innocent humans were "able not to sin" *(posse non peccare),* humans cracked by sin are "not able not to sin" *(non posse non peccare).*

Augustine was convinced that because of our inborn cracks of ignorance and weakness of will, none of us can live an entire life free from sin *(Sermon 181, 1).* The ordinary human being, indeed every human being, will fall short of the perfect life. The best that humans can accomplish is to more or less stumble through time and enter eternity in a slightly charred condition. They will have "survived" rather than conquered. And this is how they survived. They perhaps enjoyed sexual pleasure too much, but they were never unfaithful to their spouse. They did not always bear injury or insult with equanimity, sometimes becoming enraged and desiring vengeance. Still, they were willing to forgive if asked. They would not think of stealing from others, but they would fight fiercely in court to protect their property. They were quick to admit the evil they had done and humbly thanked God for helping them to do some good. Augustine firmly believed that these are the survivors John spoke about in the book of Revelation, the ordinary saints who eventually will be welcomed into the company of the healed blessed who reign in heaven eternally with Christ *(Against Two Letters of the Pelagians,* 3.5.14).

The beginning of salvation for these slightly singed souls is in humbly admitting they are indeed cracked. To do this they need to be cured of the misconception that they do not need the help of God to change their lives (*Sermon 130a*, 6–9). For them to pretend otherwise would be both disastrous and silly. It would be like going into a doctor's office and pointing out what is right rather than what is wrong (*Commentary on Psalm 32/2*, 12).

But such an admission of weakness is not always easy. Often we hide ourselves from ourselves, creating false images of our self because we are afraid to look at the reality of our warts and blemishes. Honesty is therefore essential and warrants serious reflection before going further in our search for our true self.

## The Need for Honesty

Consider, my friends, how difficult it is for people to go home when they have a disruptive home. They rush downtown with enthusiasm, but when the time comes for them to return to their own house, they get terribly depressed. Going to their home means facing aggravation, recriminations, fighting, and turmoil. When there is no peace at home among those who live there, the house is disorderly and there is a natural desire to run outside. Well, if people are miserable going home, afraid to face their family's wrangling, how much more miserable are those who are reluctant to face their own conscience, afraid of being overwhelmed by the strife arising from their sins (*Commentary on Psalm 33/2*, no. 8).

The first step in discovering our true selves is to make a firm decision to be honest. There is no question that looking at our "inner self" can be a frightening thing, more frightening by far than those poor folks who declare on talk shows, "I hate my body!" and plead for some expert to "make them over" or "make them up" so they might be free of the horror of seeing themselves in the morning mirror. As far as I know, no one has ever appeared declaring "I hate my soul," begging for a spiritual makeover that could erase the scars from their past excess, that could cool the fever of hidden passion. Unfortunately, there is no one who can do such repairs to our internal complexion except ourselves, and before we can do that we must get over the fear of looking at ourselves.

Augustine was firmly convinced that even in his better days (when he was a respected and faithful leader of the African church) he did not have a clean record. He knew that to be a truly good person one must not only avoid evil actions; one must avoid even the desire to perform evil actions. In civil law you cannot be condemned for what you think, but in God's eyes evil is not simply a matter of deeds done. As he warned his friends, "In God's judgment it is also a matter of thoughts thought" (*Sermon 170*, 3).

This creates a real problem for those striving for perfection. Augustine believed that we all have lustful or covetous appetites. The only change he noticed was that when the fires of lust begin to dim, greed begins to grow (*The Good of Widowhood*, 20.26). Externally we may seem to lead a quiet life worthy of respect, but inside we may still entertain disreputable desires not fit to be seen. The law tells us not to take another's goods (be they riches or people), and as long as we covet them but don't grab them the world thinks of us as fine people. But inside, where we nurture inflamed desires for the person or property of others, desires seen only by God and ourselves (if we have the courage to face up to them), we are not as fine as we sometimes pretend to be (*Sermon 170*, 5).

Denying the truth of our own imperfection, we may begin to think that we *are* indeed fine people and that our virtue is our own doing. Having achieved our own view of perfection, we may just settle in to enjoy the view as we look down upon the horde of disreputable, weak-kneed sinners below us (*Sermon 170*, 7). This is truly a sad state, worse even than if we were enthusiastically profligate. The reason is simple: we can make no progress toward God if we are convinced we have already arrived.

There are two ways to avoid the issue of our own "crackedness." We can fool ourselves into seeing an inner self that is not really there, or we can simply not look at all, fearing that we will find only emptiness and corruption and be faced with the horrifying conclusion that this is *me!* It is so much easier to drift along on the surface of our own life and pass judgment on the lives of others (*Sermon 19,* 2–3). There is no real surprise in this. We feel no guilt when we consider the sins of others. We do not get disgusted when we review someone else's trash. But when we begin to consider our own dank depths, to remember our past depravity, to confront our own degenerate desires, such revelations can cause us such terror that we are willing to go anywhere and do anything to get away from the sickening sight of our selves.

Certainly none of us who have lived any length of days has a completely clean inner self. For all of us (who have any honesty and sense) there will be some guilt for past evils freely chosen. For all of us (who still have any remnants of passion within) there will be embarrassing desires that escape police action only because they are unexpressed. We may still feel the delight that comes from the presence of some sexually attractive "other" even when our delectation is somewhat morose due to our inability to pursue it.

For all of us who have not completely lost our sense of self-worth there will be fetid pools of pride-filled hurt feelings that bubble with periodic eruptions of envy, anger, and desire for revenge. Of course, when we look inside our selves, there are usually some good things to be found also, but the bad we find seems to capture our attention more. Perhaps it is because when we slog through a swamp it is difficult to appreciate the clear blue sky above.

One thing is certain: true happiness can only come from recognition of the truth. This is the reason lying is insanity, at least lying to ourselves and trying to lie to God. Some teachers of ethics argue that telling an untruth (a euphemism for lying) to another person is sometimes justified if the other has no right to the truth. Others go further, justifying misrepresentation (another euphemism for lying) if the other person would be harmed by the truth, if they cannot handle it well.

There is no question that this reason justifies withholding the truth from another when telling would do no good in general and would do harm to the person told. If others cannot rationally deal with some truth about ourselves (for example, that we hate them or have been unfaithful to them), out of charity we should not force the truth upon them. Sometimes marriages are preserved by not knowing the indiscretions or even affairs of one's spouse. In such cases ignorance is at least peace, if not exactly bliss.

But such excuses for lying make no sense when speaking of telling the truth about ourselves to ourselves or to God. In the search for my real self ignorance is not bliss. It is foolishness. I am what I am whether I like it or not. Attempting to lie about myself to God goes beyond foolishness. It is insanity. God already has the truth about me, and the only reason God wants me to admit that truth (be it bad or good) is for my benefit, not for God's information. Indeed, the reason we are sometimes unable to say "I'm sorry!" is not because we worry about shocking the divine Listener. Rather, it is because we do not want to admit our malice to ourselves. Once we proclaim it, we can no longer ignore it and must then do something about it. Perhaps that is part of the therapy of the sacrament of reconciliation. By speaking our sins anonymously into the ears of another, we are forced to put into words the warts and wounds of our self that we have so often glossed over.

Through confession we no longer hide the bad parts of being ourselves. We hang them out for ourselves to see, and in that action we demonstrate our sorrow more powerfully than our words can express. God must smile when we do it because God knows better than we do that knowledge is the beginning of contrition and contrition is the beginning of salvation. God forgives us because we have taken the first step in forgiving ourselves. We no longer are playing the game of "liar, liar." We have moved away from fantasy into reality.

Admittedly, it sometimes takes great heroism to face ourselves, but this we must do. It is in our inner self that we will find the person we actually are, not the person we sometimes pretend to be. It is in our inner self that we will find our beauty, our timelessness, and our value. It is only there that in this life we will come closest to the God who made us in the likeness of God's beauty, who made our spirit to be immortal, who gave us our surpassing worth by valuing us through God's love. And the best part of all this is that when we enter into ourselves and humbly accept the fact of our imperfections, we find no one to condemn us (*Sermon 169*, 18).

# Part 2

## *Obstacles to Self-Discovery*

The psalmist sings: "My God, as the deer longs for brooks abundant with water, so does my soul thirst for you" (Ps 42:2). To drink of this fountain an inner thirst must first be kindled. We should follow the example of the deer, which will destroy serpents that hinder its progress. After it kills these poisonous obstacles, its thirst for the refreshing brook waters becomes even more intense. The serpents are our vices. If we overcome these evil vipers, then we will long even more for the Fountain of Truth (*Commentary on Psalm 41*, 2–3).

To discover our true self we must first eliminate those obstacles that stand in the way or distract from our examination of self. Like the deer seeking the refreshing brook waters of enlightenment, if we do not clear away the poisonous "serpents" (distractions and vices) that stand in our way, we will never be refreshed. It is logical, therefore, to say something about some of the obstacles (the "serpents") that may hinder our progress before considering more of the facts about "self" revealed by an unfettered investigation. The obstacles considered in the pages that follow are these:

1. earthly attachment,
2. concupiscence of the flesh,
3. avarice,
4. concupiscence of the eyes,
5. earthly ambition,
6. the "make-believe" self.

# Earthly Attachment

> In this life there are two loves in conflict in every temptation: the love of this world and the love of God. Whichever one wins out draws the lover like gravity in its direction. It is not through feet or wings but by desire that we come to God. And it is not by some physical bond or iron chain that we are bound to earth. We are bound simply by our desire for the things of earth (*Sermon 344*, 1).

Despite what some have said, it is not because we are a fallen race that our existence is so deeply embedded in the material world. This is the way it was meant to be. We are creatures of matter and spirit, and that is what we shall be eternally. To live in space and time flows from our human nature; to be so engrossed in this world that we are unwilling to look beyond it comes from our being "cracked."

The obstacle to our perfection that is chronologically first in our individual history is this *attachment to earthy things*. We are not born infected with pride or despair or lust or avarice. Nor as infants do we have the vices (hatred, envy, jealousy) that warp human relationships. We are all born like little animals, carnal beings deeply involved in and pleasured by the material things around us. In the beginning our joys and sorrows are limited to the pleasures and needs of the body.

There is nothing wrong in this. As babies it is natural for us to reach out to the food and drink and physical comfort we need to survive. However, to continue such a life of earthy, lusty desire eventually becomes a matter of choice. Some never seem to make that choice. They are content to live out their days seeking nothing but good food, good drink, and the pleasures that come from satisfaction of every bodily desire (*Letter 140*, 2).

Food, drink, and generally feeling good are our first loves, and in themselves they are not evil. Indeed, through such pedestrian loves we give our own modest reflection of the Creator, who is love itself and who made us beings who could love, beings who were created to desire. The question for us is thus not whether we should or should not love. The question is, what do we love and how much do we love it?

We have been given the power to love so that we could desire and love God, the ultimate good, which when possessed brings happiness. But this need to love God was never meant to prevent loving other things in a fitting way. Indeed, such love is expected, since every object has its own degree of goodness and is worthy of its own degree of love. The problem is in going too far in our love for such passing things. As Augustine remarks,

> God gave us all these created things to love but we should love the One who made them more. If you neglect God out of love for the world he made, is not such love a kind of adultery? (*Commentary on the Epistle of John*, 2.11.1–2).

This world is good because it was created by a good God, and therefore the delight that comes from living in the midst of this good world cannot be evil. Augustine is quite firm in his insistence that it is not evil to seek the pleasures that come from marriage and children, nor is it evil to wish to protect the welfare of those we love (*Letter 130*, 5.11). It is not wrong to seek in the world positions of honor and authority as long as they are sought for good reasons (*Letter 130*, 6.12). It is not wrong to seek the necessities of life for oneself and one's family, to provide for one's health, to seek that clothing and ornament that allows one to live honorably and respectfully in accord with one's position in society (*Letter 130*, 6.12) as long as one in so doing does not neglect the needs of one's soul (*Sermon 161*, 11).

Finally, it is not wrong to seek to have friends or to seek safety for them and for ourselves (*Letter 130*, 6.13). Indeed, fine friends and personal safety are among the few goods we seek for their own sake and not for the sake of obtaining some other good. But at the same time, they are goods for this time and place and should not be sought with such passion that our personal salvation is jeopardized. It is a grand thing to live safely on earth, but it is better still to live safely through eternity. It is a wonderful thing to have a human love, someone united to us in a bond of friendship, but such a human love cannot stand in the way of the friendship we are meant to have with God.

And so it is for all earthly goods, whether (to use Augustine's colorful analogy) it be

> . . . gold, the jaundice of earth,
> . . . or silver, the wanness of the world,
> . . . or honor, the smoke of time.

These things are transient goods that will soon disappear. They are no more lasting than a diaphanous mist that is quickly dissipated (*Sermon 19*, 5–6). No wonder that loving things of earth too much brings its own special misery! The only thing that lasts is the guilt of realizing we have disrupted our life here and endangered our life hereafter because of our foolish passion. As Augustine warned his friends:

> When we sin for the sake of an earthly good we experience a special misery when we realize that we must leave all behind when we die. The only thing we carry into eternity is our sin. Do you sin to accumulate money? The money must be left here. Do you sin in order to acquire some grand piece of property? It must be left behind. Have you sinned out of passion for some human being? They must be left here (*Sermon 58*, 9).

To love money or property or another human being too passionately does not make *them* evil. But it can have many disastrous effects on the one who too enthusiastically loves them. The pleasure of possession quickly dissipates as the earthly thing passes on. And the pain of loss is great. As Augustine observes, the unfulfilled passion to acquire a good does not hurt as much as losing a good that was for a time possessed (*Sermon 318*, 2). What he is saying is that it is *not* true that it is better to have loved and lost than not to have loved at all. The pain of seeking a good not yet achieved is at least softened by hope; the loss of a cherished love carries with it the agony of great expectations forever shattered.

The river of time in all the beauty of its changing forms moves on through its established course, taking with it those things imbedded in space and time that we possess and love just now. It is then that we come to realize the foolishness of our passion. We supposed this material thing, this physical ecstasy, that so delighted us was indeed the most important thing in life, the final goal that would bring us perfect happiness. We said to ourselves, "This wonderful moment in the stream of the days in my life is what is meant by heaven. All I need do is to extend it infinitely." But this we cannot do, and we weep at its passing (*On True Religion*, 20.40). Perhaps it was this truth that prompted Augustine (on an obviously bad day) to suggest that the very fact that we are born crying rather than laughing seems to predict the troubles that come from being embedded in this world (*City of God*, 21.14).

One of the burdens of living a purely earthly life is that we can become earthy (*Commentary on the First Epistle of John*, 2.14.5). We become tired as we rush about on the circumference of life ignoring the center of our lives, that point of unity that makes sense of the flowing multiplicity that circles around us. The most important place of God in this world is in the individual soul, a person's inner self. This is the center of the circle that is our reality. When the soul devotes itself to the things of the world, it is as if it deserts the center of things and spends its time wandering around the circumference of life far from God and its true self. The soul thins out its resources moving from this delightful passing good to the next. It is battered by the flow of temporal things and becomes exhausted.

In its search for the unity that exists only at the center, it is worn out by its pursuit of the glittering goods apparently waiting for it on the fringes of life. In the words of Augustine:

> The soul extending itself out beyond its center is pummeled by the immensity of the passing crowd of things. It is like a worn-out beggar whose nature forces it to seek everywhere for "that which is one" but is hindered in its search by the very multitude it sees passing by (*On Order*, 1.2.3).

Certainly, we must deal with and serve the passing world in which we live, but too much emphasis on the practical needs of here and now can make us lose sight of the eternal destiny that lies before us (*The Trinity*, 12.8.13).

If we are totally enmeshed in the world that we perceive through our senses, it becomes difficult to return to our true self, that self deep inside that cannot be sensed, only intuited (*On Order*, 2.11.30). Such is the power of the exclusive love of external things, that we become stuck to them with the glue of care, worrying about accumulation of more and more, worrying about the maintenance of what we have, worrying about losing anything we now call "mine"—my house, my money, my spouse, my child, my lover.

Even when we try to return to our inner self, we drag these external things along through the images of them we form in our mind. So powerful are our images of these external goods, these things that exist in the material world of space and time, that we come to define our self in their terms, saying, "I am what I possess! I am my things!" When we think of ourselves in such material terms, our true self becomes forever hidden (*The Trinity*, 10.2.7; 10.3.8).

In some way or other we must lift ourselves beyond earth to discover the self and the God who sits silently within. If our heart stays trapped on earth it will simply rot. It must fly to the heavens in its desire if it is to preserve its integrity (*Sermon 265c*, 1). This world of space and time will not be forever. Now is the time to ask ourselves, "Am I infatuated by this world or not?" It is even now falling apart, and we must learn how to let go of it before it lets go of us in death (*Sermon 125*, 11).

It is natural to be ecstatic when daily life is filled with pleasure and to be upset when it is filled with pain, but some bitter days are good for us. Augustine observes that just as a mother will sometimes spread a bitter lotion on her breast to break her infant of dependence on the comfort of suckling, so too the foul taste of some of the days of this life should move us to become detached and to look for a better and higher life somewhere else (*Sermon 311*, 14). But whether the days are good or bad, all we can do is accept them and perhaps follow (if we can) Augustine's somewhat animated advice:

> Let us wave aside with disdain whatever delightful but passing things this world offers! Let us treat with scorn whatever harsh and horrid threats it bellows at us! (*Sermon 304*, 3).

There are many good effects of such detachment. No longer enslaved by the passing things of this world, we become free to love God. It is a fact of psychology that the less we cling to what we consider our own, the more will we be able to cling to others (*The Trinity*, 12.11.16). In the words of Augustine:

> God comes to the hearts of men like a farmer seeking land to possess. If he finds it covered with woods, he roots out all the trees. Once he has a clear field, he plants it with the tree of divine love. What are the woods that stood in the way? Nothing else than the excessive love of this world (*Commentary on the First Epistle of John*, 2.8).

# Concupiscence of the Flesh

## The Problem

> How many evils are caused by our craving for the "pleasures of the flesh"? It is the root of adultery and fornication, dissipation and drunkenness. It is the source of all those things that illicitly pleasure the senses and poison the mind with their toxic sweetness. The result is that the spirit becomes the slave of the body, the master becomes subordinate to the servant. In such a condition how can anyone live an upright life when their inner self is so upside down? (*Sermon 313a*, 2).

Despite what Plato said, it was not because of some primordial failure that we have a body with so many mundane desires, desires that seem so commonplace when compared with the spirit's thirst for truth and beauty. The fact that we have a body is not an imposition on our spirit. Indeed, Augustine believed that our soul has a natural need to live in our body, a need created from the very beginning when God made us rational animals, beings composed of a material body and a rational spirit united (*A Literal Commentary on Genesis*, 7.27.38; *On Continence*, 10.24; 8.20).

Having a body, we are indeed quite different from our angelic cousins, those pure spirits standing before the throne of God. But being different does not make us lesser creations. Through the union of our soul with our body we reflect the goodness of God in our own special way, and in doing so we are truly good. Indeed, along with the angels we are the best part of creation.

It follows that the various desires we have because we have bodies cannot be evil in themselves. It is not because of sin that we get hungry and thirsty, that we react positively to physical comfort and negatively to physical pain. These desires (which we share with the humble animals) have a good purpose: to keep us alive. So too our desire for sexual union has a good purpose: to keep the human race alive. The fact that all of these desires can sometimes get out of control, can take over our lives, does not make them evil. It simply points to the fact that the regulating power, our spirit, is a bit cracked.

Augustine would be the first to agree that the so-called desires of the flesh can sometimes take over our lives. His desire for sexual satisfaction and his inability to control it delayed his conversion to Christ until his early thirties, and he freely admitted that the sexual urge was sometimes powerfully reawakened throughout his subsequent life. Perhaps he remembered his early years when he was "in love with love" as he wrote these words:

> Sexual passion sometimes does not just affect the body. At times it takes complete control of the whole man, both physically and emotionally. It causes the most intense erotic pleasure, a pleasure which at the peak of its ecstasy practically paralyzes all power of deliberation (*City of God*, 14.16).

Augustine admits that he did not always have control over his sexual desires, but at the same time he maintains that the sexual drive and its satisfaction through the act of intercourse does not become evil because it is sometimes so difficult to control. Its primary natural effect intended by God, the creation of children, is a great good. If Adam and Eve had remained in the paradise described by the Old Testament book of Genesis, Augustine had no doubt they would have produced children in the same way as they did after their fall from grace, by an intimate physical union between two humans who loved each other deeply. The only difference would have been that in paradise their love for each other and God would have controlled their physical passion (*City of God*, 14.14; 14.10; *A Literal*

*Commentary on Genesis*, 11.42.59). Augustine firmly believed that the act of coitus is not evil in itself. It becomes wrong only because it is performed in improper circumstances or with immoderate passion (*City of God*, 14.18).

In Augustine's usage "concupiscence" is a neutral word; it means simply "desire." Even when it refers to physical passion it does not necessarily denote a condition that is sinful. Emotional reaction to the pleasant and unpleasant in life is part of being human. Apathy is not the ideal state for the human being; controlled fervor is. In Augustine's view, the apathy championed by the Stoics as the perfect human condition was worse than any vice (*City of God*, 14.9). Even when the phrase "concupiscence of the flesh" has a negative connotation, it refers not to a longing of the body but to a disorder in the will (*Against Julian the Heretic*, 3.9.18).

The real obstacle to our perfection is not *concupiscentia*, simple desire. It is the *libido,* or lust, by which we prefer any temporal good to eternal goods (*On Lying*, 7.10). It is this lust that causes a human being to enjoy any creature with such exclusive passion that God is ignored (*On Christian Doctrine*, 3.10.16). Since the good desired can be anything temporal, it would be a mistake to interpret the phrase "the flesh lusts" too strictly. Although it may sometimes refer to sexual desire, it can refer to any realm where the person's desire is out of control (*City of God*, 14.15).

Because we are cracked, the temptation to go overboard in seeking to feel good will be with us as long as we live, and often it is hard to overcome. Dreaming of physical pleasure sometimes holds our attention more powerfully than quiet meditation on wisdom. On some days sexual fulfillment seems so much easier than the joy that comes from a complex balanced love for another human being. On some days the pleasures of good food and good drink are more immediate and easier to achieve than the pleasure of solving a geometry problem. On most days the aroma of a well-cooked meal seems more enticing than a life of harsh asceticism. People tell me there is an exhilaration that comes from the performance of a noble act of self-sacrifice, but just now the pleasure of a long nap seems more attractive.

In an odd way our immoderate "fleshly" desires some-times seem to express our basic wish for life, meaning, and love. For example, we can mistakenly believe that our thirst for *life* begins and ends with feeling good physically, with the ab-sence of hunger, thirst, and pain. We can make the mistake of believing that our thirst for *meaning* can be satisfied by the ac-cumulation of things or by the number of victims we conquer in our sexual escapades. Some of our promiscuous adventures, frequent and fleeting sexual relationships, are sad attempts to find true *love*.

Whatever the reason, our unruly desires for the pleasures and things of time can create a serious obstacle to discovery of our true self. It is therefore important to consider what the remedy might be for our sometimes impetuous "concupis-cence of the flesh."

### The Remedy: Friendly Asceticism

> Why is it of benefit to abstain sometimes from food and from physical comfort? The reason is this: our flesh tends downward; our spirit tends upwards. Our spirit is drawn to the heavens by love but it is slowed down by the weight of its body. Thus our fleshly desires are like earthy luggage which is a load on the soul. Such ballast must be cast off if we are to rise unfettered to the heavens. This is what we do when we fast (*The Usefulness of Fasting*, 2).

Assuming our soul has its own house in order, it must exer-cise some sort of control over our body (*Sermon 169*, 1). We are *rational* animals, and it makes good sense to demand that our spirit should have some control over the desires of our body. It is not that there are two warring adversaries inside us. It is just that we are a union of body and spirit, and therefore the total amount of energy we have is limited and must be expended judiciously to serve the needs of both. Too much exuberance in pursuing the pleasures of the body may exhaust us.

There is only one desire that can be pursued without restriction, and that is the desire for God. Truthfully, such desire does not tend to take over the lives of most of us just now. Great saints may be passionate about God all the time, but most ordinary folk like me (and perhaps you) have passions that run in other directions. Most days I worry more about having a good meal, not getting sick, not being alone, than I do about whether I shall see God just now. Of course, I hope for eternal salvation (and sometimes even work to achieve it), but just now I am satisfied if the air-conditioning is working and I am not in too much pain.

Augustine subscribed to the view that when we limit the fulfillment of the joys of our body, there is the chance we will develop even more joy in the spirit, replacing lust for a lover with true love, replacing drunkenness with the intoxication of understanding what is true and what is good, overcoming boredom not by dulling the mind with fantasy but by reflecting on the list of the truly good things in life, things like "relatively good health, . . . friends to call upon in need, . . . the promise of future immortality, . . . the assurance that God will help in our struggle for salvation if asked" (*The Usefulness of Fasting*, 5).

Augustine believed that healthy denial of bodily demands can expand the space in our "self" for more and greater goods. We are stretched by our unfulfilled desire and gain a greater capacity for the good we truly need (*The Usefulness of Fasting*, 1). When we are "filled up" with earthy goods that will not last, we lose our desire for anything beyond them. Full to the brim with Thanksgiving turkey, for a time we desire nothing more.

This does not mean we should ignore our body's legitimate needs (*On Christian Doctrine*, 1.26.27). In my experience it is hard to do philosophy or theology on an empty stomach, and when a person's stomach is empty for too long it becomes impossible to do anything at all. To die of starvation is not the way of the cross that Christ spoke about. It is entirely natural and worthwhile for our bodies to seek those goods necessary to preserve life on earth. It is natural for our spirits to seek heavenly goods that are infinite and permanent. Our problem comes not from our desires for such different things. Our troubles come from the cracked machinery (our mind and free will) through which we desire and pursue such things.

This is the reason our appetites are sometimes in conflict. Even assuming our spirit knows it is meant for heaven and has some recognition of the way to get there, our body remains like a young horse prancing here and there, following any and all delights that tempt it to wander from the right path. Because of the wildness of our bodily appetites, we must train them for useful service as one might train young colts, using reins that are neither too slack nor too firm in order to channel their natural vigor toward the good (*Confessions*, 10.31.47; *The Usefulness of Fasting*, 3.3).

Of course, the difference between us and wandering horses is that in our case the wandering is not the fault of our steed (our body) but of our spirit. In our case it is not so much the horse that needs correction as it is the rider, who freely chooses either to let his body drag him wherever it wishes or destroys his faithful friend by undue beatings and denial of true needs.

When we come to think about it, we begin to realize that asceticism is needed more by the soul than by the body. The troubles of life come not from bodily urges but from the spirit's consent. Sin is not in the inclination but in the consent to the inclination (*On Continence*, 2.3). Sin is not in the desires of the body; it is in the choice of our spirit to seek satisfaction of those desires in some untoward way. Augustine points out that one may dress modestly with the hope of controlling sexual urges, but the virtues that effect such control are in the soul.

Whatever our ascetic practices may be, they are not as important as what is happening inside us. No matter how virtuous our activities may appear to others, no matter how others wonder at the severity of our ascetic life, it has no value if, for example, charity is lacking within. Augustine puts it plainly:

"How can your fast (or your abstinence) have any good effect if you ignore your fellow human being?" (*The Usefulness of Fasting*, 5). Simeon Stylites was a saint not because he sat on a pole in the middle of a desert but because in his ascetic hermitage he was consumed by love for God and neighbor.

We are meant to have bodies as much as we are meant to have souls. The Christian teaching on resurrection tells us this. Christianity also tells us that in heaven when we get everything back together (a now glorious body united again to its shining spirit) things will be just fine. We shall finally and forever be at peace with our bodies (*Sermon 155*, 14.15). But just now things are not always so fine. Our imagination sometimes will sweep over our spirits with suggestions, fantasies, and dreams that we are ashamed to admit even to ourselves. Our body is still a friend, but it is a rambunctious friend that will need cautious care as long as we are here. As Augustine warns, "While our body moves along shakily in this life, while it is still burdened with the weight of day-by-day existence, it sometimes has its own moments of rebellion when it is truly dangerous to our spirit" (*The Usefulness of Fasting*, 3).

For most of us riding through time on this rowdy steed that is our body, a "friendly asceticism" is at times a highly recommended practice lest we fall off the right path.

# Avarice

Avarice is insatiable. For example, a person owns this farm but he wants to get possession of another farm that he does not own. Wanting to become even more rich he is ablaze with desire. Like someone who suffers the raging thirst of dropsy, the more he drinks the thirstier he gets. The avaricious have dropsy of the heart. When you have dropsy in your body, it becomes filled with fluid. It is endangered by all the fluid it has but it never seems to get enough. This is exactly what happens when you are avaricious. The more you have, the more you seem to need. When you had less, you wanted less. You could enjoy your life with fewer things and you were thrilled by the small sums of money you had. By being filled up, you have become stretched by your affluence to the point of obesity but still you go on drinking and being thirsty for more and more (*Sermon 177*, 6).

In the previous reflection on concupiscence of the flesh the emphasis was on the desire for the pleasures that come from the fulfillment of bodily appetites. Here we consider the delight we have in possessing *things*. Pushed to extremes such desires become the vice of *avarice*. In its broadest meaning avarice means seeking more than is sufficient to meet our needs (*Commentary on the First Epistle of John*, 8.6) and can include the excessive thirst for any material or spiritual good (*Sermon 107*, 8 and 10). Thus it is possible to be avaricious for knowledge or fame or human love or wealth.

Taken more narrowly, avarice applies only to the desire for this last good. It is the immoderate desire for money and all that money can buy. Augustine considered such excessive desire for material possessions one of the major obstacles to discovering the self and God. It begins with a desire for a "something"; it ends with a desire for "everything." A man begins by wanting a little farm and ends up craving everything in heaven and on earth (*Commentary on Psalm 39*, 7).

It is not unnatural for us to desire to use and own material things. Even in a perfect world ownership of things would be a rational way to regulate fair use among a multitude of people. As long as we live on earth we will always need to use things. We must have food to eat, water to drink, shelter from the changing weather. We desire material things in this world not because we are cracked but because we are human. We crave the things of this world, we make possession of such things our one goal in life, because we are cracked. The obstacle to our discovery of self and God is not our *possession* but our *passion* for material things. As Augustine remarked, there is no advantage in standing before God with nothing in your hands if your heart is consumed with the desire for everything (*Commentary on Psalm 51*, 14). The evil of avarice thus comes from inordinately wanting to be rich, not from being rich (*Sermon 85*, 6).

Augustine believed that when persons sacrifice love of God for the sake of love of themselves and then feed that love by greedily grasping earthly things, they lose not only God but themselves. Consumed by the pleasures of the external world, the food and drink, the honor and power, the apparent respect and love that money can buy, they lose all incentive and indeed all ability to look seriously at their inner self. Happily blinded by their reflection in the mirror of the things they own and the purchased honors and love they enjoy, they are no longer able to see themselves as they are.

Their situation is not unlike my childhood fantasy when I frequented the wonderful fun house on the boardwalk at Wildwood, New Jersey. A scrawny, somewhat ugly child, I loved to stand before the wonderful warped mirrors that seemed to make me bigger and more handsome than I was. When we base our lives on the image reflected by our wealth we get the same sort of distorted image of our true selves. We say: "See how worthwhile I am; I own so many things of worth! See how loved I am by those who flock to me to share my wealth! I must be first class because I can always buy first-class accommodations wherever I go in life!"

Believing such things, we escape to things beyond ourselves, leaving behind not only the God within but our true self that lies hidden within. In our passion to accumulate more and more external goods, we ignore the plaintive call of conscience seeking to limit our unbridled lust for things. We become like the prodigal son (Luke 15:17-19), choosing wealth over the love of our Father. In such a state

> Love of money has caused you to destroy yourself. You tell lies on account of money. While looking for money you have destroyed your soul. You now value things more than yourself (*Sermon 330*).

In the story of the prodigal son, the young boy stopped his flight from his father and himself only when his money ran out. It was his salvation that he seemed to be more interested in having a good time than in hoarding his wealth. He was infected with extravagance more than miserliness. Of course, both the spendthrift and the miser are driven by an inordinate obsession with wealth, but their motives are quite different. The wastrel wants more and more so he can spend more and more. The miser wants more and more so he can possess more and more (*Sermon 86*, 6).

Forced to choose between these two moral maladies, being a spendthrift seems to be less deadly. When the money runs out, the spendthrift has a chance of coming to his senses, as the world that had been so captivated by his spending rushes off to find another foolish pigeon. This is what happened to the prodigal son. He had lived the high life, but when the money ran out, he was reduced to feeding pigs (*Sermon 330*, 3). Free now from the possession and, more importantly, the *desire* for possessions, the boy was able to *return to himself* and thereafter return to his father. As long as he had been living outside himself in the money and goods he owned, he was unable to see himself. Unable to see himself, he was unable to even think about his father, God. Augustine takes a lesson from the story and applies it to all the avaricious:

> God justly reproaches all those souls who go away from him by choosing wealth in place of him. God says, "You thought, if you withdrew from me, you would have more" (Isa 57:8). You discovered that, like the prodigal son, you have ended up feeding pigs. You have lost all things. You came back to yourself and your Father only when you got tired of being in want (*Sermon 177,* 10).

It is hard to be converted from our lust for things when we are in the midst of enjoying them. Immersed in the good times of our lives, the pleasure of our possessions can take over our lives. Perhaps Augustine was describing his own adolescent days of immersion in earthy pleasure when he wrote:

> Our spirits become swollen with the fun of living on earth, and we find it almost impossible to even think about matters relating to God. We are consumed by our daily experiences of this earth, and we find it extremely difficult to lift our sights again to the affairs of God (*Letter 95,* 2).

Sometimes this unthinking enjoyment of the things in our life goes sour when we begin to experience the tension of living a life where success is measured only by accumulation. The tension caused by the daily need to "make it" can become suffocating. As Augustine put it to a friend:

> I cannot help thinking that the turmoil caused by violent storms in wilderness, twisting us this way and that, is easier to bear than the strife we are called upon to fear and endure because of our day-by-day involvement in the affairs of this world (*Letter 95,* 4).

In truth, possessing things is not an unmixed blessing. Augustine believed it was because of disputes over property that this life is so filled with "lawsuits, hatreds, discords, wars, disagreements, riots, and murders" (*Commentary on Psalm 131*, 5). He spoke with the weary voice of experience when he advised his friends:

> When someone sues you to take your coat, you should prefer to lose the coat so that you can save your time to give to God. If you go to court you will lose your peace of mind. You will become upset. How much better to lose your *thing* and save your *time* (*Sermon 167*, 3).

Despite all our efforts, our coats and things and wealth will ultimately disappear. Augustine thought it entirely proper that money should be minted as round coins since it so easily seems to roll away (*Commentary on Psalm 83*, 3). It is silly to live and die in the pursuit of money. If you have lived only for its accumulation and preservation, both it and you will perish when you die (*Sermon 335c*, 7; *Sermon 299f*, 5; *Sermon 38*, 6). You may say, "Well, rather than lose my money I will take it and buy a country house. There I will be buried and I will continue to possess it." To this plan Augustine gives the sardonic response: "If you are buried there, indeed something paradoxical will happen. Your property will then have *you*; you will not have *it*" (*Sermon 335c*, 8).

There is no question that at death we shall finally be unattached (if not detached) from our earthly wealth. In Tolstoy's powerful story *How Much Land Does a Man Need?* the greedy farmer who dies in his frantic effort to get more and more land finds in the end that he needed only about six feet. But such detachment of the dead is hard to come by while still dwelling in the land of the quick. We are drawn to things because we are ourselves things. We feel safe with things. We like our things because they concentrate our attention on the here and now, narrow bits of reality that we think we can understand and control.

Detachment from this earth is difficult because it is frightening to fly, to gaze into the "not yet" or "what possibly might be." It is a fearsome thing to look to an unexperienced heaven when we have yet to understand our experienced earth. It is a task for the gods, but that is precisely what we are called to be. We are called by the Lord to become like God. But we cannot be filled with God if our hearts are filled with the desire for things (*Sermon 177*, 4; *The Trinity*, 12.11.16).

How silly we are! We forget that no matter what we possess, someday our life will end and all our "things" will be left behind for others to haggle over. Whatever good things we may enjoy in this world, be it health or money or honor or indeed even love from fellow humans, all of these passing things are just smoke and wind. All things of this world rush down the river of time toward the dark sea of oblivion. To attach ourselves to them too firmly condemns us to the same fate: an eternity in the darkness of separation from God (*Commentary on the Gospel of John*, 10.6.2). Thus the advice of Augustine makes very good sense, if ever we could absorb it and follow it:

> You are now in an Inn for travelers. Use wealth as a traveler in a wayside Inn uses the table, cup, pitcher, and couch in his room, all those things that must be left behind when we continue our journey (*Commentary on the Gospel of John*, 40.10.2).

# Concupiscence of the Eyes

What vulgarity is caused by our sometimes shameless curiosity! This is what has been called "concupiscence of the eyes" and is sometimes exhibited in our eager craving for frivolous shows and spectacles. Consider the madness of the coliseum where the fans often begin fighting in the stands! At least the people on the field compete for some prize. What prize is there for the crowds who fight in the stands over their favorites? They become ecstatic over this or that player. They go to shows cheering for their favorite actor on the stage. And then they have the effrontery afterwards to piously proclaim: "Those players on the field or on the stage are truly disreputable!" But tell me, are those who watch any less disreputable? If they did not buy the tickets, there would be no indecency, no violence for sale. When you patronize such shows, you establish the shameful business more firmly than ever. Why encourage something you find fault with? I would be very surprised if the defilement of the people you are captivated with does not rub off on you. These wretched unfortunates (those in deathly combat for your pleasure) have been made slaves to the desires and insane pleasures of those who watch. When you refuse to watch such spectacles, you are showing kindness to those who suffer violence or degradation for your pleasure (*Sermon 313a*, no. 3).

This quote from Augustine shows that times do not change that much. Like the people of his day, we sometimes are overcome by curiosity about what is happening around us. Augustine used the phrase "concupiscence of the eyes" to describe such excessive curiosity, and he considered it to be an obstacle to self-discovery because when overindulged it leaves no time for reflection on what is happening inside ourselves.

It is a deathly curiosity when it distracts us from the important fact that we "have not here a lasting city," that we are on the road and need to keep our attention focused on where we are going and how we will get there. Heaven is not a gift coming to us with no effort on our part. We must want it and work for it, and we work for it by giving serious consideration to what we are, who we are, and how we stand in terms of our eternal destiny. Our natural curiosity drives us toward the truth that will eventually lead us to happiness with God, but as long as that curiosity is directed exclusively to the people and things around us the discovery of such truth becomes impossible.

There is nothing inherently evil in being interested in the lives of others, in playing at games, in enjoying shows. Indeed, one who loses all interest in this world is not acting in a healthy fashion. Such apathy may be the sign of a deep-rooted depression that sees no good in anything or anyone. We are beings who are drawn naturally to the beauty of art, the thrill of competition, and the wonder of the lives of other human beings. It is only when these interests take over our lives that they become obstacles to self-discovery. Obsession with the passing flow of events, with the fantasy world of creative imagination, prevents us from looking deep into ourselves to see who we really are. Our fixation on the present passing parade stands in the way of reflection on our future and the eternity that lies ahead.

As was the case for our desire for physical comfort and a modest amount of wealth, it is not because we are a fallen race that we are so curious about the things around us. We were created with a need to know everything about everything. What is out of order is our sometime inability to focus on the truths about reality and ourselves, which are crucial for our salvation here and now. We can become so mesmerized by the unusual we forget who we are and where we are going. We become like the poor fellow on the superhighway, so intense in gaping at the accident in the other lane he forgets where he is going and indeed even forgets that he himself is still plunging down a dangerous road. His immoderate curiosity soon results in his own destruction.

To be honest, one of the reasons for our fascination with the trivial is that we get bored easily. Perhaps this is because we have been created with a thirst for nothing less than the infinite beauty, infinite goodness, and infinite pleasure that comes from possession of the infinite God. With such an infinite thirst it is not surprising that even the best things in life begin to lose their zest eventually. Even saints are not exempt. Augustine went so far as to suggest that the special trial of the saintly is a boredom in living the virtuous life day in and day out (*Commentary on Psalm 106*, 6).

Moreover, living with a demanding body and a sometimes dulled mind, we have difficulty in focusing for any length of time on any issue that is the least bit abstract, subjects like "our destiny," "our nature," "good and evil." Some pundit with a sense of humor once said he would rather experience concupiscence than be able to define it. After forty years of teaching philosophy I know what he was saying. Our present condition is such that it is difficult for us to concentrate on ultimate truths over a long period of time. Frankly, there were days when teaching philosophy was just as boring as learning it. Indeed, there were even days when writing about spirituality lost out to TV presentations of the foibles and fables of the passing scene. The descriptions of the "dark night of the soul" seemed less distressing than the dark screen of the broken cable TV.

On most days it is hard to hear God's whispers because we are deafened by the rushing waters of our lives, the passing events and the shouting people that surround us. When we search for salvation in the babble surrounding us, we will sometimes join any new group that seems interesting. We give up our traditional faith because "we do not get anything out of it." Its teachings are hard to understand and live by; its celebrations are drab and dreary. How much nicer to be with a group who dance and make no demands!

Sometimes our curiosity drives us to peer inordinately into the lives of others, especially those odd people who surface on afternoon talk shows. Consumed by interest in their peculiar problems, we have no time to devote to our own destiny, our own weakness and strength. This phenomenon one day led Augustine to cry out to his listeners:

> We truly are hopeless creatures. The less we concentrate on our own faults, the more interested we become in the faults of others. We love to criticize others and spend little or no time correcting ourselves. We cannot stand looking at our own disreputable lives but we are quite eager to pass judgment on everyone else (*Sermon 19*, 2–3).

It does seem to be part of our present cracked condition that we have an almost irresistible temptation to gossip about the foibles of others as we float with them down the river of time. Our own life seems so dull by comparison and there seem to be so many truly outlandish things happening to others. There are so many interesting "others" to examine and comment on that it seems we simply don't have any time to think about our own wandering selves. We do not realize, as we merrily watch the sinking lives of others, that our own life is in danger of sinking into the depths from all of the accumulated bilge water of greed, anger, lust, and downright meanness that is ours alone (*Commentary on the Gospel of John*, 12.14.2; *Sermon 56*, 19; *Sermon 77b*, 7).

We forget the truth spoken by the Old Testament prophet: "Our own faults are revealed as soon as we open our mouth to pass judgment on others" (Sir 27:4). And so we spend our days talking more and more about less and less, thereby demonstrating the emptiness within and the accuracy of Augustine's observation that the people who do the most talking are often those who have the least to say. Their talk reverberates loudly in space only because it is amplified by the echoing chambers of their empty head. It would be better indeed (as Augustine adds) "if such people would keep their 'fiddle-faddle' to them-

selves and learn from the wise rather than converse with fools"
(*City of God*, 5.26).

In our quiet moments we may come to realize the importance of spending more time searching for our real self and
thinking about our destiny, but the problem is that our quiet
moments are few and far between as we wander here and there
through the sounds and sights of the world around us. We become interested in stories about others rather than facing honestly our own story. We dedicate all our time and effort to
earthly projects, new towers of Babel that we hope will make us
immortal and ensure our legacy (*City of God*, 16.2-10).

We become excited about combat on the playing field and
ignore the continuing combat inside ourselves between what
should be done and what is pleasant to do. We laugh and cry at
fantasies and ignore the reality of our own life. Even Augustine
was not exempt from such vanities. Writing about his experiences as a young student, he admits that he often sacrificed his
studies in order to win at games and that he developed an in-
creasing curiosity about adult shows (*Confessions*, 1.10). Later
on, when he was formally exposed to the great literature of his
day, he became even more captivated. He writes:

> I was forced to memorize the wanderings of Aeneas (whoever
> *he* was) while forgetting my own wanderings; and to weep for
> the death of Dido, who killed herself for love, while bearing
> dry-eyed my own pitiful state: the fact that I was becoming
> dead to You, O God. Nothing could be more pitiful that a
> pitiable creature who does not see to pity himself, one who
> weeps for the death that Dido suffered through love of Aeneas
> and not for the death he suffers himself through not loving
> You, O God (*Confessions*, 1.13).

Though he himself was never addicted to the games and
races of the coliseum (his friend Alypius was), he saw the mad-
dening effect such competitions and shows had on the people
of his church. As we read the following harangue he addressed
to his parishioners as they shuffled uneasily waiting for the
Sunday service to be over so they could rush to the coliseum or

theater, it is easy to think of the scene at popular rock concerts or contentious football games:

> On all sides the seething crowds, the hubbub of people converging on the stadium, pointing out the posters to each other as if it was all something tremendous, working themselves up to a pitch of excitement, touting the trivial attractions, urging one another to go, to see. To go where? To see what? To a place where witless fools can go and return even more mindless (*Sermon 142*, 7).

Augustine was not saying it is always a waste of time to spend some of our days engrossed in theater and literature. Nor was he saying it is wrong to go to athletic contests and cheer for our team. What is wrong is when these fantasies and contests take over our lives, when our curiosity for these externals consumes all of our attention.

This (in Augustine's opinion) is precisely what happened to the prodigal son. The beginning of the boy's downfall was his overpowering curiosity about what the world "out there" was like (Luke 15:14-15), what answers were being given by astrologers, soothsayers, and secular masters to the meaning of life. In the words of Augustine:

> Such wrongheaded curiosity led to a poverty of truth. The son, torn away from his father (God) by the insistent hunger of his mind, began to feed on the husks of earthly teachings, husks which crackle and pop but do not satisfy, husks which are fit food for pigs but not for human beings (*Sermon 112a*, 3).

As long as the boy was consumed by curiosity about the husks of passing things, he was unable to appreciate the eternal. He was living outside himself and thus was unable to find the God who dwells not in the fantasies and games of the passing scene but in the depths of the inner self.

Considering all this, it becomes clear that the danger of the obstacle called "curiosity of the eyes" is not that it makes us do bad things; it is that it diverts our attention from doing the good we must do in order to successfully make our pilgrim way to our Father's house in heaven. It is a dangerous temptation because this world is indeed an interesting place. And so it should be because it is, like us, a reflection of the wonder that is God.

# Worldly Ambition

> The world retains its hold on us, on all sides its charms decoy us. We like lots of money, we like splendid honors, we like power to scare others. We like all these things, but let's listen to the apostle: "We brought nothing into this world, neither can we take anything out" (1 Tim 6:7). Honor should be looking for you, not you for it (*Sermon 39*, 2).

**W**orldly ambition *(ambitio saeculi)*, sometimes called "pride of life," means much more than the simple desire to *make something* of ourselves in this life. As the phrase is used in Scripture and by Augustine, it stands for the malignant desire to be important on earth and to be prepared to use any means to achieve that end.

It is malignant in a number of ways. First, in the choice to make fame or power on earth as its only goal, it leads to that "second death" described by Augustine as the eternal separation from God. Second, it is malignant in its willingness to sacrifice morality and other people in pursuit of its selfish goals. Finally, it is malignant in that it destroys a balanced perspective on this life. It promotes the insanity of pride, the belief that we are the most important beings on earth and that our supposed position of eminence has been accomplished purely through our own efforts. We come to believe that (despite what is sometimes unkindly whispered by others) we do *not* have a superiority complex. We in fact *are* superior.

Throughout history humans have taken one or more of the following three paths toward worldly success:

1. through *accomplishing a significant work*, a work that I do which brings satisfaction to me and prompts praise from others;
2. through *acquiring a position of power* whereby everyone else is subordinate to me as superior;
3. through *accumulation of wealth* in a society that measures success in this way.

As noted in the reflection on greed, the accumulation of wealth can be good or bad, depending on what it does to us and what we do with it. As we shall see, the same can be said of "doing a great work" and "acquiring power." Each will have positive and negative aspects.

It is natural for humans to strive to *have some meaningful "work,"* a work of some importance at least in our own eyes and hopefully in the eyes of others. Thus it is a noble task (I believe) to try to put my thoughts down on paper, and it is even better when those thoughts are found worthy of publication or at least of dissemination among friends. As creatures gifted with creative imagination we are meant to use our God-given abilities to improve the world around us. To those who ask "Why does not God do something about the evil in the world?" the only logical answer is "God already did, by giving human beings the intelligence and free will to make the world a better place." We are meant to act for the good of the universe and the good of our neighbor. A human being who simply exists is a limited person at best, and when this inactivity is the result of a selfish choice, it is wrong. Existence without action is evil in a human being with normal abilities and opportunities.

The great good work that we do (or try to do) is the only way in which others can come to appreciate us. No one (except God) can see what we truly are in the depths of our inner self. We express who we are to others only by what we do. This is unfortunate, because it creates the danger that when we are no longer able to *do* we may be judged to be of no value by others and (worse still) even by ourselves. It is truly sad when a person comes to believe they are no longer worth anything because they are able to do nothing.

The Christian faith insists that we are important not because of what we do but because of what we are: special reflections of the infinite good that is God. And this faith also reminds us that as long as conscious life remains, there is always *something* noble that we can do. Everyone may not be capable of great works of intellect or imagination, but everyone is able to love. As Augustine says, our true value comes from what we are and what we love, not by the supposedly great works we do (*Sermon 313a*, 2). Unfortunately, in a world that seems to value "doing" over "being," it is sometimes hard to be convinced of this consoling truth.

Another danger that sometimes follows from "doing great works" is that we may become complacent, not caring whether we are appreciated by others or even whether we are approved by God. If we are too satisfied with our lives and works we may ignore the fact that what we may think is wonderful is no great accomplishment at all. Thus a man who measures his greatness by the number of his sexual conquests may never come to see that his morality is that of a bison in heat.

When the works we do are truly good, we may believe we have created (or at least merited) the wonderful powers that brought them about. Our pleasure with our wonderful gifts may even cause us to grasp them jealously to our breast, refusing to share even a part of them with others (*Confessions*, 10.39.64). In all these instances our good works (far from being a path to heaven) have become an obstacle, not because of what they are in themselves but because of what they have done to us.

We must indeed strive to do *grandiose* good works in our lifetime, but we must not take either their accomplishment or their absence too seriously. Great books go out of print and eventually disappear. Great discoveries are quickly superseded by even greater discoveries. And if perchance nothing exceptional comes from our best efforts, our success in God's eyes will be based on our humble efforts to do the best we can with the powers and opportunities that have been given us. We must try to do great works, to use our abilities to do great things here on earth, but in our doing we should heed the voice of Paul:

> Whatever you do, work at it with your whole being. Do it for the Lord rather than for men, since you know full well you will receive an inheritance from him as your reward (Col 3:23-24).

What has been said about seeking fame through doing great works applies also to seeking positions of authority in society. Augustine believed there was nothing wrong in accepting and even seeking such positions. He believed those with the necessary talents had an *obligation* to seek higher office so they might be of service to others (*City of God*, 5.24).

If we have the qualities that make for a good ruler, we must be careful not to refuse the crown too easily. When others look to us for leadership only to find we have humbly chosen a leisurely retirement to pursue wisdom, it is likely they will begin to question the value of a wisdom that has stolen one so qualified from their service (*Reply to Faustus the Manichean*, 22.58). As Augustine himself knew from experience, it is never easy to give up the peace of a cloistered life for a position of authority. The challenge to be in charge is the final burden placed on the lives of good people who are already well on their way to perfection (*Commentary on Psalm 106*, 7).

Desiring to take on a position of power is thus a good thing when it is desired in order to bring good to the society. It does, however, carry with it dangerous temptations. We may come to believe that to be a ruler on earth is an ultimate goal with nothing better worthy of desire. Put simply, in our desire to rule the earth, we may lose all interest in becoming a citizen of the "City of God." We may come to believe with the creators of the tower of Babel that building with earthly stones will raise us up to heaven (*City of God*, 16.2–10). We may come to believe that because we are in charge we somehow or other are now better as a human being than those over whom we rule, forgetting that we are still fragile, contingent creatures despite our temporary control over the life and death of others (*Sermon 313a*, no. 4).

The motivation behind our sometimes desperate efforts to do great things or take on positions of power or accumulate great wealth may be quite complex. Sometimes our ambition to make a mark on this world is independent of the reaction of others. If we are satisfied with the work we have accomplished, if our exercise of power or accumulation of wealth has made us a VIP (very important person) in our own eyes, we could care less what other people think of us. It is true that such narcissistic self-satisfaction is rare. Social animals that we are, most of us would like to have some affirmation from our confreres, some praise for what we have done.

Like success, whether praise is good or bad depends mightily on our reaction to it. Augustine gives a somewhat crude analogy for situations when praise is indeed a good thing. He remarks, "What a belch is, you see, to the rumbling stomach, that's what praise is to the satisfied heart" (*Sermon 255*, 5). His point is that when the heart is full, it expresses its fullness joyfully in praise, just as a healthy belch is sometimes the aftereffect of a fine meal. If we receive praise from some who are truly moved by the decency of our lives, it is a good praise in that it reflects the fullness of their hearts, a fullness to which we have somehow contributed (*Letter 231*, 4).

If others praise us for filling them up with good things, that is splendid and is rightfully savored. Unfortunately, praise from others sometimes is bestowed for less noble reasons. Sometimes the source of their praise is ignorance, praising us for the wrong thing, or for imagined virtues like

> . . . being a pleasant person who has no strong opinions about anything;
> . . . being a person of power who can bestow benefits if flattered and inflict punishments if criticized;
> . . . being someone who "goes with the flow" of society even though the direction is evil.

In these and similar cases, the "belch" of praise is but a gaseous indication of the emptiness of a heart that cannot appreciate true value.

Still, to be honest we enjoy praise whatever its source. We seem to have a natural thirst for an affirmation from others that we are indeed people of value. The excessive thirst for praise can create a problem if we begin to value the praise more than the good work we have done to earn the praise. As Augustine observes, we like to hear the words "Well done! Well done!" and to be feared, if not loved, for our power and our deeds. We begin to rejoice more in the wonder of our self than in the wonder of having God-given gifts to perform splendid deeds. In short, we seek the pleasure of being feared and loved not because of God's gifts but so we can claim that we are gods ourselves (*Confessions*, 10.36.59).

Augustine admits that it is difficult for anyone (even himself) to know whether they are free of the inordinate desire for praise (*Confessions*, 10.37.60). He recognized the truth of the statement from the book of Proverbs (27:21) that "Our daily furnace is the human tongue." Whatever we do, we are tempted to look around to see if anyone appreciates us. And it is hard to eliminate this tendency. We can take a vow of poverty to combat greed. We can vow celibacy to control our lust. But how can we give up praise when the praise comes from others and not from ourselves? And even if we could give up praise, another danger lurks. We may now seek praise from others because of our new status as a truly saintly person who has knowingly and freely taken a vow of indifference to praise. In short, we have become humble and are proud of it (*Confessions*, 10.38.63).

It is sad when our self-respect depends on earthly accomplishments wrapped in the praise of others because all worldly honors are like rising smoke, becoming thinner and thinner as they disappear into the heavens (*Commentary on Psalm 36/3*, 14). The happiness we receive from the treasures of earth are as ephemeral as a sleeper's dream (*Commentary on Psalm 131*, 8). When all the celebrations are over and our worldly crowns have been taken away, we remain what we always were: just a human being (*City of God*, 5.17). No matter how noble or successful our career has been, all will be swept away in the "River of Babylon," that ever-flowing river of time (*Commentary on Psalm 136*, 3).

What then will be the measure of my success on earth? It may seem as though I have spent a lifetime twirling about doing pedestrian things of little or no importance. If supposedly I am so great for having done great things, what do I have to show for it? After so many years I look back and see that my life was useless in making any great impact on the world. It seems to have been a tiny existence in the immensity of an uncaring world.

How then can I measure the value of my self? How can I measure whether my life has been a success? The secular world suggests three possibilities:

> 1. I could measure my success *by my job*. But it seems as though I have spent my days going through the motions in a job that appears now to have been a waste of my time. When I left one job I was not replaced. When I left another, they phased out the job. In other jobs I was succeeded by others who did the job much better than I.
>
> 2. I could measure my success *by those who have loved me*. But they are fast disappearing, either dead or busy about other loves and other things. Once we may have been close, but now it seems that I have fallen out of their circle of interest.
>
> 3. I could measure my success *by my possessions*. But what I have gathered over time has now become an encumbrance and is deteriorating faster than my aging body.

In this life only memories and a good conscience last and perhaps only these will be the measure of my success. I will be a success, then,

> . . . if when I come to the end of my time, I have a conscience that is mostly clear;
> . . . if when I stand at the beginning of eternity, God remembers my life on earth with a smile.

# The "Make-Believe" Self

> The whole message contained in the command to the mind to "know itself" comes down to the following. The mind should be certain that the "self" does not have any of those qualities which in fact are *not* present and does have those qualities which in fact *are* present (*The Trinity*, 10.16).

In the search for one's true self, Augustine makes an interesting distinction between what we "think" we are and what we "know" we are. We often create bloated and glorious pictures of ourselves, fabrications based on what we would like to be or what we dream we actually are. At the same time, sometimes hidden deep within ourselves, there are those facts about ourselves that we indeed know about ourselves but try to avoid because they are unpleasant or humbling.

Sometimes this strategy of avoidance does not work. Our hidden passions force themselves upon us at moments of weakness or vulnerability. For example, we may pretend to be virtuous people in complete control of our passions, but then we meet an attractive friend and are overcome by powerful fantasies that excite carnal passions unbecoming in polite company. We smile gracefully at the object of our affection and pretend our interest is a purely platonic pursuit of ideas, whereas in fact it is more like an epicurean thirst for pleasure. We pose as a philosopher while denying to ourselves the feelings of a lecher. We deny within us the imperfections (the "cracks") in our inner self which should tell us (if recognized and humbly accepted) that, despite our angelic pretensions, our bestial passions are never far from running wild. Augustine was well aware of this tension within himself and admitted that it was only the grace of God that prevented him from committing every sin recorded in human history and even creating a few new ones that had yet to see the light of day (*City of God*, 22.22.1).

There is often a big difference between what we *think* we are and what we should *know* we are. We may *think* that we have arrived at the pinnacle of virtue but we should *know* that the only thing standing in the way of our supposedly saintly self from becoming a satyr is the providence and grace of God. We may *think* we are not getting old, but we should *know* the truth of the matter each morning as we try to lift our resistant body from its arthritic sleep. We may *think* we will never die, but looking at the constantly passing tide of time around us and feeling the gradual deterioration inside us, we should *know* that each day of life is a step toward death. We may *think* that someday we will be wealthy, that someday we will control the world, that someday we will find the true love of our lives, but we should *know* that all of these are only possibilities, and some of them are quite remote.

The difficulty in distinguishing fact from fiction about our self is grounded in our creative imagination. This is the power whereby, from the memory of the various sights and sounds of past experience, we construct images of things that never existed and events that never happened. In my imagination I win races I never ran; I win applause I never experienced; I hold in my arms loves who are barely aware of my existence; I indulge in heroic acts that were never performed. From my memory, that power that Augustine calls the "stomach of the mind," I regurgitate and reassemble images of a life I wished to live but never achieved. In my imagination I can see many suns, although there is only one. I can make the places of my past as large or as small as I choose and indeed make new places out of bits and pieces of places I have seen or heard about. So too I create imaginative pictures of myself, pictures that have little to do with my reality. In the beginning they may be pleasant illusions; taken too far they can become insanity (*The Trinity*, 11.14).

Such creative imagination or inventive thinking is caused by the power of our will. We *choose* to unite a "this" with a "that," each of which has an actuality separate from the mind and whose union exists only in the mind. There is a reality called "beauty" and a reality called my "self," but my "beautiful self" may be a wish rather than a fact (*The Trinity*, 11.17).

It is thus we can *think* of things that never were and will-fully *forget* nasty things that actually were. It is easy to do. In order to forget, all we need do is not pay attention. For example, sometimes (especially at long meetings) people talk to us, and we have no idea what they are saying because our minds are elsewhere. Our mind must have the permission of our will before it can pay attention to our present or remember our past (*The Trinity*, 11.15). It is not difficult to forget when others tell us how rotten we are and to remember only their praises. Indeed, such selective attention and remembering may be the source of much of our daily peace.

Sometimes our lack of attention to self is caused by things outside our selves. We can become so captivated by externals that we lose awareness of our self and the God who resides deep in the self. As Augustine describes it, we go away into exile from ourselves by not paying attention to what is inside out of love for what is outside (*Sermon 330*, 3).

Sometimes these externals can become so important to us that they are worshiped as idols. Augustine accused the pagans of his time of doing precisely that. They created idols of gods with all the passions and perversity of human experience and then formed their own self in the likeness of those idols by acting like them (*Sermon 23b*, 5).

The reason for this is that our inner self has a full range of natural desires and needs, and sometimes it is tempted to turn outside to find its satisfaction. It turns its back on itself and on the God who resides within and reaches outside to things such as drugs or drink or ambition or money or fulfillment of its most basic animal desires for food, drink, and sexual satisfaction. By uniting ourselves with such things, we lose sight of our true self and become like its idols: unthinking, uncaring, uncontrolled in passion. It is tragic when this happens because the only good worthy of worship is the God who lies hidden deep inside our own true self. As Augustine counseled his people, "First come back to yourself from the things outside you, and then give yourself back to the one who made you" (*Sermon 330*, 3).

In the course of our life we may create or remember many "selves" that have only minimal connection with reality. I once attended a meeting of philosophers (an assembly where odd ideas are not only expected but even demanded) where one speaker suggested that, rather than worrying about discovery of self, all of us should face the fact that in our time on earth each of us lives many lives and many deaths. His claim was that in this one span of time that is our life now, we have not had one self but many selves: an infant self, an adolescent self, a mature self, and so on. In his view our lives are not united by one continuous self but rather by a succession of separate selves following one upon the other.

It is true that at least some of our past self-existences are gone from consciousness. As hard as it is to face up to my present "geezer" self, I find it almost impossible to remember my infant self. Seeing my self is not always easy, but remembering my self has become more an exercise of creative imagination than true reminiscence. At best it is selective memory, capturing bits and pieces of the self in accordance with a plan not devised by me but by psychic forces beyond my ken or control. My dreams (night and day) perhaps reflect this. They are based on my past experiences and past encounters with others, but the picture created by them has little to do with the reality of how things were. I mix together remembered places and remembered friends in combinations that never occurred in reality. Old loves suddenly appear in strange places. Old events are rewritten to suit my present paranoia or desire.

Places are remembered differently too. Going back to the house where I was a child, the seashore boardwalk where I gamboled as a youth, the room where I lived in college, I am surprised by how small they actually are. Perhaps I remember them as large because my memory of that long-ago self is of a diminutive self, a self of no special importance. But now, in my memory, that past self sometimes appears grander than it was, a huge self that hogged the stage of its times. In these memories of my past days I often appear at the center of every action. In the fantasy and fallacy of my creative imagination I am always the head of the class, the most important person in my love's life, the great performer on the stage of life, whereas in truth I was a less than diligent scholar, a passing fancy in the lives of many whom I loved, an invisible, huddled listener in the rear of life's theater.

This creative remembering of a self that never was is an innocent diversion as long as it does not stand in the way of seeing myself for what I am now. My self is not only my present state but also my past history, and misrepresenting the latter can be just as destructive as ignoring the former. Like it or not, I am a continuum, and an understanding of what the true ME is now rests on an honest awareness of my past. I am my history, and to see myself now I must try to remember honestly what I have been, as disconcerting as that memory may sometimes be. Like Augustine in his *Confessions*, I must not hide from myself the foibles of my youth or the passions of my adolescence or the excesses of my young manhood or the thirst for fame and power of my productive years because the residue of these past times, be they good or bad, remains a part of my self now: the vices overcome and virtues developed a sign of present strength, the passions still unconquered a sign of present weakness.

Indeed, the nobility of my present self is created as much by vices conquered as virtues maintained. It is good to remember that and not to live my days as a "make-believe" self. The miracle of my present true self is that I have somehow survived my history without too much damage to my self or others. Facing my self past and present honestly, I can be thankful for the folly that might have been while regretting the stupidity that sometimes was.

# Part 3

## *On the Road to Discovery*

Don't let's soothe ourselves with flattery; let us weigh ourselves up, and tell ourselves the truth. Why do you expect to hear it from me? You yourselves must tell yourselves the truth. I've simply arranged to put a mirror in front of you, in which you can all look at yourselves. I'm not myself the reflective power of the mirror, which can show those who look into it their faces. The faces I'm talking about now, you see, are the ones we have inside us. I can address them through your ears; I can't see them. Certainly, I'm presenting you with a mirror; look at yourselves, each one of you, and tell yourselves what you see (*Sermon 306b*, 4).

With a humble awareness of where I have come from and the wounds that history has inflicted on me and with a cautious attempt to avoid the obstacles that could stand in the way of self-discovery, I am now prepared to say something about what I know from faith and experience about my true self. It will be far from a full picture. I will need an eternity not only to gradually come to understand God but even to understand myself. But at least in beginning I am moving toward that vision of God and myself that I thirst for.

# The Grace-Filled Self

The law given by God is good because it tells us what we should do and what we should not do. But if people believe they can fulfill the law on their own without the aid of the grace of Christ, their presumption is useless and harmful. Therefore it behooves the exhausted sinner, knowing that he does not have the strength to change his ways, to call for the help of the Savior. Then he will be given the grace which forgives past sins, assists his own efforts to conquer present sin, and bestows a love of righteousness. This does not mean that all temptations of the flesh against the spirit will cease, but if the spirit is firmly based in the grace and love of God, the person will not give in and sin (*Commentary on the Epistle to the Romans*, 13–18).

Augustine did not need to read Scripture to discover that he was "cracked." He had established that fact by his own life, especially the years before his conversion. During much of his early life he had wandered, not knowing what he should do, sometimes living the sensual life of an unthinking pagan, moving from the mysticism of the Manichees to the ethereal views of Neoplatonism, ending finally in a skepticism that rejected any answer as certain. Later on he made his first tentative steps returning to Christianity and began to see the truth that there was an action-guiding law—the commandments revealed by faith and confirmed by the voice of reason deep within.

The problem was that, while before he could excuse his wandering life on the basis of ignorance, now he knew what he should do and was fully responsible when he did not do it. He came to recognize the second aspect of the cracks left in him by sin, his inability to consistently choose the good he knew he should choose. As time went on he also discovered the reason why, despite his weakness, he was *sometimes* able to do the right thing. It was because he was not only cracked, he was also grace-filled. He came to realize that he was not alone in his battle to reach his ultimate end, perfect happiness with God in heaven. He had help from God not only to *know* the right thing to do but to *choose* to do it once known.

The amazing thing about this divine intervention was that it left him free. It had its effect by giving him the *power to love* righteously. This, along with God's providential arrangement of the circumstances of life, helped him choose to perform the good acts that would move him along the path to salvation. How could such powerful divine intervention *not* cancel out his freedom? Augustine hints at the answer in his famous declaration: "My love is my weight. Wheresoever I go, it is my love that pulls me there" (*Confessions*, 13.9,10).

This is more than a pious thought. It is a factual description of the process of free choice. For choice to occur there must first of all be *love*, a love that is created in us by the presence or promise of *delight*. We love because we are *pleased* to love, pleased either because we see that the object of our affection is good in itself *(amor benevolentiae)* or because we experience some benefit from it *(amor concupiscentiae)*. The reason we choose anything is because we *know* it, *delight* in it, and finally *love* (that is, *desire*) it. Any action of an external agent that creates or enhances a person's internal knowledge, delight, and love does not destroy their freedom but empowers it. I never believed that in my years of revealing the mysteries of ethics to my students I was forcing them to be ethical. When someone gives me a recent picture of my loved one, they do not force me to love; they enhance my love by drawing my attention to the delightful beauty I had forgotten.

In the same way, the fact that I am grace-filled does not mean I am freedom-empty. As Augustine remarks:

> Does grace destroy free will? Just the opposite. It creates it. It makes the will healthy so that now it can freely love the moral life. Grace makes the will healthy so that it can love righteousness freely (*On the Spirit and the Letter*, 30.52).

We cannot choose something we do not know, but neither will we choose something that does not delight us. In the passage above Augustine's point is that through grace we are led to delight in goods that before never attracted us even if we knew them. We speak in ordinary life about olives and the octopus and other odd things as being an acquired taste. So too is it with the moral life. Although we may know the moral law naturally (it is imprinted on our spirit), in our cracked condition we are not automatically drawn to observe it, especially when it is difficult to do so. The taste for the good life must be acquired, and this is precisely the effect of grace on our spirits. It gives our spirits the taste for the "good life," not as defined by society but as defined by God, and then supports us in reaching out to this newfound good that has suddenly delighted us. This infusion of delight comes not from education or new experiences or conversation with a friend. It comes directly from the Holy Spirit, the Third Person of the blessed Trinity.

Augustine's reading of Scripture revealed to him the following truth:

> Fulfillment of the law is nothing else than love and God's love is created in our hearts not through our own efforts but by "the Holy Spirit who is given to us" (Rom 5:5) (*Nature and Grace*, 17, 18).

And again:

> The beginning of love is the beginning of righteousness; progress in love is progress in righteousness; great love is great righteousness; perfect love is perfect righteousness. It is not "poured out in our hearts" by nature or by our own choice but only "by the Holy Spirit who has been given to us." The Spirit comes to the aid of our weakness and along with us restores our good health. This love is nothing else than the grace of God

through Jesus Christ, our Lord (Rom 7:25) (*Nature and Grace,* 70.84).

It is clear that Augustine's description of grace goes far beyond the analogy of a helpful crutch given to us as we limp along on the path to heaven. Grace does more than simply strengthen our powers of choosing to walk the right path. It *makes* us walk. It not only "lifts us up" to that high road to heaven, it makes us run up that path. Grace, in sum, not only enables us to choose and do the good, in a sense it *compels* us. But how can it compel us to choose and not destroy our free choice? Augustine freely admits that humans cannot resist the will of God. If they are unwilling, God *makes* them willing. True Christians are *driven* to love God by receiving the gift of love from the Holy Spirit.

A possible explanation might be developed along the following lines. As long as the will is not *pushed* to do "X," it may be said to be free with respect to "X." To be "drawn" by "X," attracted by "X," does not destroy freedom. It establishes its conditions. This image of "being drawn" is precisely the image Augustine uses in describing the action of grace on the will. He uses the example of the fierce warriors of Israel choosing the young boy David as their king. He asks:

> How did God induce them to choose David? By tying them up in chains? By no means. He worked inside them. He moved their wills and *drew* them to choose David in such a fashion that they chose freely (*Admonition and Grace*, 14.45).

He goes on to say that if God has such power over humans in the choice of a king, it would seem reasonable to say he would have power to bring a human to conversion. He cites the example of the conversion of Peter to make this point. Peter came to Christ by first having the Father "reveal" the truth of Christ to him. Did this do injury to Peter's freedom? Augustine uses the following analogy to prove that it did not:

> Show a green branch to a sheep and you will attract it. Show a child some chestnuts and you will attract it. Both are drawn by

their love. They are drawn not by bodily torture but by the desire of their heart. If it is true to say that everyone is drawn towards that which pleases them, can we deny that Christ is able to draw a person towards him in the same way? (*Commentary on the Gospel of John*, 26.6.5).

Since God had created the person who is Peter to be a free being, it certainly is not beyond possibility that God should be able to work through that free will to move Peter from being unwilling to being willing. The tools for such influence are present in the knowledge, delight, and love that fuel the engine of free choice. A sheep cannot desire a green branch that it cannot see. A child will likely turn away from chestnuts if it has already gotten sick from eating too much. But is it remotely possible that Peter could turn his back on Christ once he *saw* and *delighted* and felt the *love* that had been drawn from his heart? It is extremely unlikely. Indeed, Augustine would say that it is just impossible. But this does not make Peter any less free. The knowledge is still his; the delight is still his; the love welling up in his heart is still his. It was because of his own knowledge, delight, and love that he gave up his nets and ran down the path after Christ, supported and drawn irresistibly by the grace of God.

Does such divine action take away our dignity as human beings? Does such grace-filled intervention somehow lessen our responsibility for our destiny? Augustine certainly did not think so. He told his people that God made them without their cooperation but God would not save them without their cooperation (*Sermon 169*, 11.13). There is nothing to lose in having our wills "drawn" by the will of God. Indeed, as Augustine suggests, "our free will can do nothing better than to submit itself to *being led* by the God who can do nothing wrong" (*On the Works of the Pelagians*, 3.5).

Indeed, at the end of time when finally we see God face to face, we may come to realize that the heavenly delight by which God "drew out" our free choice was the best thing that happened to us in life. Even now, with our "cracks" in mind and will still plaguing us, we should be able to see that it is better to put our faith, hope, and love in God rather than in ourselves. It just makes good sense to depend on the will that is stronger (*On the Predestination of the Saints*, 11.21). It just makes sense to submit oneself to one who loves us infinitely more than we can ever love ourselves, one who created us with the fervent wish that we might be all together in a land where love and delight are unending and where we are finally and forever free.

One final point. Once we recognize the fact that our lives are indeed grace-filled, we never again should think we are alone in this life. The words Augustine addressed to his friend Italica consoling her after the death of her husband are just as true for each one of us: "You must not think of yourself as left alone. Christ lives deep inside you and is present in your heart through faith" (*Letter 92*, 1).

# The Fragile Self: Rising Smoke

> Do you wish to know what you are when you are on your own?
> Do you wish to know what you can accomplish with no outside
> help? The psalmist tells you exactly: "His spirit left him and he
> went back into the earth. On that day all thought of him per-
> ished" [Ps 146:4]. This is what you are when there is nothing in
> you but yourself! (*Sermon 335b*, 4).

It does not take long in my search for self to realize that
my self is fragile. Every existing human being is a "something"
pulled towards nothingness. As the song from the musical
*Porgy and Bess* reminds us, "We ain't necessarily so." Augustine
remarks that in a way we are more brittle than glass. A glass
goblet can last for centuries if properly taken care of, but "we
are so brittle that even if we are not destroyed by accident, we
still cannot live very long" (*Sermon 17*, 7.7).

We are not like a house that can remain even after the
builder departs. If God should lose sight of us, cease to pay attention to us, we would instantly go out of existence (*A Literal
Commentary on Genesis*, 4.12.22). Neither are we like a field that
can support life once it has been plowed and fertilized. We are
more like luminescent air, fighting to retain the light that makes
us sparkle. We cannot shine on our own. We escape the dark of
non-existence only so long as divine light stays with us and in us.
When we have distanced ourselves from God, we are consumed
by darkness. God is still inside us. He has not gone to some other
place, but we have turned our backs on him as we seek salvation
in some non-god (*A Literal Commentary on Genesis*, 8.12.26).

Augustine describes our existence here on earth as being more fragile than a spider's web. A web is secure as long as it is not touched, but we cannot continue to exist unless we are touched and supported by a force beyond us (*Commentary on Psalm 38*, 18). We are something like party balloons temporarily expanded to enhance a festive gathering. The delicate air of "being" easily escapes if not preserved by the gentle pressure of God's hand. It is for this reason that Augustine described our earthly lives as fleeting as rising smoke. In a sermon he told his listeners that, though it is true that the promise of heaven invites human beings to "choose life and seek the joy of good days" (Ps 34:12), the fact that must be faced at the present moment is this:

> You never had nor never will have such days in this life. In this life "your days are fading away like smoke" (Ps 102:3). As the days go by the self seems to become more diaphanous. As our days grow in length they become fewer. The ascending course of our days has led to their vanishing away (*Sermon 216*, 4).

This image of the self as rising smoke, beginning thick and dense and gradually dissipating as it rises through its appointed time until finally disappearing into the limitless heavens, seems quite accurate when we think about it. When we begin our existence we are thick with unexpended possibilities. Our life is dense and thick because the fire that feeds it is at its peak. Our unused bodily strength stands ready to explode us into the prime of our physical lives. Our minds, unhampered by past bad experiences or the accretion of bad habits, are eager to be exercised. They have the untapped power to seek the truth, to create beauty, to find love. No strength has been used or wasted. It seems that we can become anything we choose.

But as life goes on we become diluted. Going in one direction closes off many others. What we do to our bodies and our spirits narrows their future. Living a great length of years makes our life "thin out." Certainly our physical strength is diminished, and sometimes our mental powers are lessened too. It is said that you can't teach an old dog new tricks, and to some extent this is probably true. The force of habit makes it difficult to change a course from a road long traveled, from a way of living or a way of thinking ingrained in us by time.

Furthermore, we "old dogs" may begin to forget those "old tricks," that insight and wisdom that had been part of our lives for so many years. In the sometime forgetfulness and reveries of a life long-lived it seems as though our self has become filmy. Our fire no longer blazes as it once did. It only smolders, rising toward the heavens as ever-thinning smoke.

This gradual thinning out seems confirmed by the reactions of those around us. When we are in our last days the world at times treats us as though we have already "disappeared into the heavens." No one approaches us for advice; no one offers us a grand new task that only WE can accomplish. If we are lucky we still have a few old loves whose affection adds to our substance, but sometimes even these are lacking. Those who care for us are paid to do so, like those assigned to watch a smoldering fire until it is at last extinguished and its final smoky breath disappears. The question for any of us in our lengthening life is whether our self will disappear from time like rising smoke or will grow in substance in the eyes of God as we come closer and closer to eternity.

Our spirit makes us desire eternal existence, but in fact we live on the edge of annihilation. It is this tension that is at the root of our continuing anxiety. We want to be something (and at times pretend to be everything) but are always on the verge of being nothing. We are born in a delicate bag of skin, a thin barrier protecting all those precious things inside that together make physical life. And even more, it encases that mysterious entity that someday will be mind, the mind that will eventually discover my self and (if I am not careful) will come to claim that my skin-bagged self is much greater than the self of everyone else. We go through our lives puffing up our selves, but all the while the delicate fabric that contains us gets no better. It only gets older and stiffer until finally it splits and spits out with a sigh the fragile self to an unknown destiny.

Perhaps it is this awareness of our fragility that prompts some of us to spend a lifetime seeking a safe place, a place we are used to, a comforting place with no surprises. If we find such a place, we can become so firmly attached that we come to believe we will never be separated from it. We come to believe we will never be cast out from our little "safe-house" to wander through time and space, floating aimlessly like gossamer dandelion seeds pulled here and there by the whimsical breeze.

My fragility is a fact, perhaps the first fact about my self that I discover if I look at my self anyway seriously. On any given day I can get up from lunch and with no warning suddenly fall into death as my spirit plummets into life beyond death. How am I to deal with this sobering fact? I can think of only three possible courses of action.

I can simply ignore it, at least as applied to myself. Over the years I have been present at more than a hundred funerals. Though some caused great sorrow, it was not because I saw in them a harbinger of my own destiny. Burying a loved one, I was sad not because I would someday die but because I was still alive and alone. Burying strangers made even less of an impact. I gave an example of the phenomenon that Augustine noted long ago, that we humans are somber as we bury someone else but quickly forget the event once it is over and never think that one day we shall be the ones buried (*Sermon 361*, 5.5).

On the other hand, I may accept my fragility and the tentative nature of earthly existence and use this as an excuse to live as I please now. I make my own the principle "eat, drink, and be merry, for tomorrow you will die!" I say to myself "After death there is nothing (or at least nothing I need worry about); I might as well enjoy myself while I am still here."

Or finally, if I have the gift of faith and hope (faith that there is a happy life possible after death and hope in a Lord who will help me attain it), I may live by a slight modification of the hedonist principle above. I will say to myself, "Eat, drink, and die, for tomorrow you shall be merry." And then I will continue to truly *live* until I die, continuing to enjoy the innocent pleasures of this life. But I will also accept my death, not as an end but as a door to a life of eternal happiness. My concern will not be to get as much out of this life as possible but to make sure the life I get out of will not jeopardize the life I will get into after death.

One thing for sure: "Life happens," and I desperately want it to be a satisfying life. But no matter how satisfying this life is, I must be ready to move beyond it. I must not reject my life now, tenuous as it may be, but also I must not be too attached. It is only reasonable for me to be ready for the thread that holds me alive to finally break. It makes sense to follow Augustine's sage advice: "Learn how to let go of the world before it lets go of you" (*Sermon 125*, 11).

Thinking about my fragility may sometimes be frightening, but there are some advantages. Who would want to live forever on this side of the grave, especially when friends and family have already crossed over? Moreover, knowing there will be an end to my fragile existence, I may come to value each day I have here in time and make it count for eternity.

## The Imperishable Self

The unbelievers say: "Let us eat and drink today because tomorrow we die!" They say this because they do not hope for resurrection. However, we who believe in resurrection must not give up hope and fall away, encumbering ourselves with drugs and drink. Rather we should wait expectantly and alertly, girding our loins and lighting our lamps in anticipation of the coming of the Lord. We should fast and pray, not because "tomorrow we shall die," but in order that we might die confidently and without care (*Sermon 361*, 21).

**W**hen Augustine was a young man at the peak of his physical and intellectual powers, he put down on paper this imaginary dialogue with Reason:

> *Reason*: Do you know that you are immortal?
> *Augustine*: I do not know.
> *Reason*: Of all the things you don't know, which would you want to know above all else?
> *Augustine*: I would like to know whether or not I am immortal.
> *Reason*: Do you love life as much as that?
> *Augustine*: Indeed I do (*Soliloquies*, 2.1).

Questioned further, Augustine declared that the reason for his desire to live forever was a more fundamental desire: the desire to continue to *know*, to be conscious of his self and its surroundings, to be able to understand himself and the world in which he lived. Put simply, he wanted to live forever so that he might continue to grow in knowledge. He was not satisfied with simply existing forever as lifeless rock or a vegetable that lived but did little more. He wanted to be immortal as a human being.

Augustine was not unique in his desire. Most human beings share his wish to be immortal. We all desire to live forever at the peak of our powers, to be imperishable with good health, complete peace, and perfect happiness. Because of this driving desire we clutch at existence, sometimes sacrificing all else for a few more moments of life. Sadly, despite our best efforts, our life on earth seems to be constantly thinning out. We are slowly but surely fading away. And so we pray for some sign that would contradict our evident frailty, some experience that would assure us that our self is imperishable.

Some ancient philosophers, ignoring the deterioration of their bodies (unfortunate appendages to the real self in their view), claimed that at least the "mind," the "soul," will go on forever. Indeed, it prospers once released from the prison of decaying flesh. They said: "The soul is something other than matter (how they argued that is another issue), and therefore it has no parts that can fall apart." They said: "The mind contains eternal truths, and so it too must be eternal."

Although such arguments have merit as intellectual exercises, I doubt that they ever brought hope and consolation to a human on his deathbed. This is so because my self, the "I" that is "me," is as much my body as it is my mind. This explains why in the stories from ancient mythologies those who had passed beyond death to live in the shadowland on the other side of the river Styx were constantly trying to return to this life. They were indeed alive on the other side of death but in a ghostly state. They were living wraiths, conscious beings of little substance. They would never again face death, but they still were unhappy. And no wonder. They had lost half of themselves, their sometimes troublesome but always beloved body (*Sermon 241*, 4).

Such is my desire for imperishable life that I cannot be satisfied with having a long life this side of death. As Augustine remarked:

Nothing that has an end is a long time. Only if your "time" has no end will I be willing to concede that it is a long time. If your time for living is limited, then I am convinced that it is brief (*Sermon 335b*, 2).

Nor can my thirst for life be satisfied by the promise that I will live on in the minds of those who loved me or that I will be "recycled" to enrich the earth and thereby nourish future generations. I do not want to be sod, I want to be saved. I do not want to be mulch, I want to be ME.

Finally, my desire to live cannot be satisfied by the prospect of my soul surviving death without my body, however pleasant that may seem. Augustine believed that the "bodyless" state between death and resurrection could be somewhat pleasant, something like being in a peaceful sleep (*Commentary on Psalm 129*, 8). The analogy does strike a responsive chord, especially for those of us whose sleep is now characterized by mini-resurrections, times of frequent risings. When we sleep we are certainly still alive, and in our dreams we do seem to live a conscious life independent of the body. Our spirits live in their own little world, a world composed of memories and imaginations flowing from experiences that are not present now. If the dreams are pleasant, then this dream-life is joyful in its own way. In our dreams we laugh as well as cry. In our dreams we love. In our dreams we feel really fine, at least until our body interrupts our reverie with its anxious call for nocturnal relief.

After death our sleep promises to be even more peaceful. We can dream without interruption because there is no body to make demands. Such a prospect is inviting, but most of us would not want it extended eternally. We love to sleep, but who would want to sleep forever except as an escape from pain? But even in this latter case, our sleeping cannot be called a true good; at best it is the lesser of two evils. Indeed, a perpetual dreaming sleep, whatever the circumstances may be, is as horrible as being trapped in an unresponsive body, a situation in which we are aware of all that is around us but are unable to break through the borders of our now useless flesh. To know that you are sleeping and that this condition will last forever comes close to the classic description of hell: a conscious existence completely isolated from all that in life was the source of your happiness.

Augustine can describe this interim between death and resurrection as being pleasant only because it is not to be forever. The soul in the midst of its drowsy existence is buoyed by the conviction that the day will come when the voice of Christ will call it forth once again into the land of light, where it will be reunited forever with its old friend, the body (*Sermon 223c,* 1).

The Christian faith assures us that eventually there will be resurrection, when our continually existing spirit will be united with a new, more perfect body. Indeed, belief in Christ's and our own resurrection is at the very foundation of Christian teaching. Without it, all of Christian doctrine collapses (*Sermon 361,* 2–3).

Augustine was puzzled by those in his day who firmly believed in Christ's resurrection but could not bring themselves to accept their own. In his view the two resurrections were tied together. He argued that if Christ is head of the mystical body and we are its members, it does not make sense to say that the "death of death" occurs only in the head and not in the members (*Sermon 233,* 4). In fact, one of the reasons for the plan to save humanity through the death and resurrection of the Son of God was precisely so that the human children of God could come to believe in their own resurrection (*Sermon 241,* 1; *Sermon 242a,* 1). Jesus-God wanted to do more than predict resurrection; he wanted to demonstrate it (*Sermon 242,* 1).

Christ's own resurrection and the various resurrections of others that he performed in his life show that resurrection is possible, at least for the recently dead (*Sermon 361,* 8). We are told that after three days in the grave Lazarus stank, but at least he was still there. To those who wondered how resurrection was possible for those long dead, those whose body had long ago disappeared into the dust of the earth, Augustine answered that to resurrect a human being who once existed was less amazing than the day-by-day creation of so many humans who previously had never existed. Like so many "ordinary" miracles, the miracle of conception is so common that it is often disregarded as being uninteresting (*Sermon 242*, 1).

Nature itself demonstrates that life springing from death is part of the very fabric of existence. Seeds must be buried before they can bloom again. The seasons of the year yield their place to what follows, only to appear once again. The moon waxes and wanes but then becomes full again. Augustine asks, "Is it then likely that humans, the most perfect image of God in creation, should not do the same?" (*Sermon 361*, 9–10).

Believing in my immortality does not make my life any less fragile. But now it appears to me not as a short thin line in human history, a mark of no consequence in the scheme of things, an existence that will cease without causing great ripples in the stream of time. Now I see it as a minute dot at the beginning of a noble line that is infinite in length. From this perspective I can see that what happens in this life is not as important as what will happen in that eternal life after death. Indeed, what I do or am in this life has importance only in how it affects what I will do or be in eternity. If I have any sense at all, I should not fear too much that first death (the temporary separation of soul from body that marks the end of my time) so much as I should fear the possibility of a second death, the eternal separation of my self from God. I should heed the advice Augustine gave long ago to his parish congregation:

> Let the self fear its own total death of body and soul, and not fear the death of its body so much. If it fears its total death and lives a life which does not offend God and thereby drive him out of its life, then at the end of time it will receive its body back once again, not to suffer everlasting punishment but to rejoice in a life that will never end (*Sermon 65*, 8).

When I was younger I liked to blow bubbles with an old pipe and some soapy water that I mixed myself. I imagined myself a creator, one who could make a beautiful "something" out of almost nothing. My bubbles were translucent beings, almost spiritual, becoming things of many colors when the light hit them just right. They would float into the sky and then eventually "pop" and disappear, leaving behind only a few drops of memory to mark their passing. When I got older I learned that their shimmering interior was held together by a thin diaphragm that separated their inside from the outside. I also learned that what was inside was about the same as the outside, the only difference being that inside there was air contained and outside there was air unbounded.

Much later I thought that this was a good analogy for the life of my self in time and eternity. I was created in a shimmering bubble of time that I was destined to color with the special gifts I had to give to the world. The bubble that was my life in time floated in an immense sea of eternity, a sea different only in its extent. That same light that brightened the eternal day also shone inside me.

One day the bubble of my time will cease to be, and that spirit that now can be seen only in the hues painted by its deeds will be set free to swim forever in the eternal sea, which for so many years had surrounded it and embraced it. I shall certainly die. My fragility predicts this. When that happens the self that is my spirit and body will disappear. But the best of "me," my immortal spirit, will endure as in a peaceful sleep, dreaming of the day when once again it will be whole, finally and forever at home with its flesh and blood.

The message of faith is that I am fragile to be sure, but I am also imperishable, a being with truly infinite possibilities. My hope is that the words Paul wrote to the Romans will someday become true for me:

> If the Spirit of him who raised Jesus from the dead dwells in you, then he who raised Jesus from the dead will bring your mortal body to life also, through his Spirit dwelling in you (Rom 8:10-11).

# The Inner Self and the Flow of Time

I hold in memory all that I have seen of sky and earth and sea. There too I discover my very self. I remember every "what" and "where" and "when" of my past actions and how they affected me. From this wealth of raw material I create images of those things that I saw or believed, and from these images of the past I think about my future . . . actions that I might perform, events that I might experience, triumphs that I might hope for. I see all these future possibilities almost as though they were present. I say to myself: "I will do this or that!" and then I actually do it. I cry out with hope: "Oh I hope that this or that will come to be!" Or I cry out in fear: "O God, don't let this happen!" I say such things to myself and the images of things hoped for or anticipated or feared are wonderfully present to me right now. Somehow or other I am able to draw them out of that great treasury that is my memory (*Confessions,* 10.14).

At the beginning of his extended reflection on time in the *Confessions* Augustine admits, "If you ask me what time is, I don't know" (*Confessions,* 11.14.17). It is easy to understand why he was bewildered. What we call "time" is made up of past, present, and future, but at this moment neither *past* nor *future* exist in any real place in this created world, a place where I can visit as I might visit the seashore or the mountains. Moreover, the *present* is only a fleeting instant that disappears as soon as I begin to consider it.

I may say that I am going to visit the many past places where I have lived (for example Wildwood, New Jersey), but when I plan to go there they are not future places and when I get there they are not past places. They are present. In a sense, the past does not exist except in my remembering, and the future does not exist except in my anticipation and hope. Without such remembering and anticipation it is impossible to know where we have been and where we might be going. Indeed, it becomes impossible to know who we are. As Augustine says in the passage above, "It is through memory that I discover my self."

Time is ephemeral at best. If time is the measure of change in terms of "before" and "after" as some philosophers have suggested, there is truth in saying with Augustine that time exists only in the mind that measures it (*Confessions*, 11.21.27). Perhaps this is the reason people talk about time in such different ways. One says that youth is a long time; another, a short time. We speak about double time and half time, and we seem to understand what we are talking about. But as Augustine observes: "These are the plainest and most common of words, and yet they are so profoundly obscure that their meaning is still to be discovered" (*Confessions*, 11.22.28).

Why is it then that we speak about a long time and a short time? Augustine concluded that no life that has an end is a long time (*Sermon 335b*, 2). Saying that "time moves fast" says more about our perception of it than about an actuality beyond our perception. Now that I am old time seems to move faster. Only when I was young did I look forward to endless summers. Now I wonder at how fast summers speed by. Perhaps this is a sign of the thirst for eternity. Time seems to speed as soon as we realize that it will someday end. As we get older we seem to measure our days more intently. If truly our summers were endless, filled with mild warmth, bright days, cool nights, and joyous celebrations with friends, if summers were an endless vacation in a pleasant place with those we love, we would not waste time measuring the extent of our days. We would simply enjoy them.

Unfortunately, this is not the way life is just now. Time is forever lost as past, forever anticipated as future, momentarily experienced as an "eye-blink" of present that quickly disappears. Indeed, it seems that the fullness of time (past, present, and future) and the richness of life exist only in our inner self reflecting on the times of our lives. Only there can we roam through all the broad meadows of our time—our past, our present, and our future. Only there can we dream of eternity.

Augustine suggests that if the mind is the brain of the inner self, the memory is its stomach (*Confessions*, 10.14.21; *The Trinity*, 15.12.22). Memory makes knowledge possible. We cannot think of something unless it is held stationary. The present is like a flash of light too swift for the eye to see; it cannot be understood until it is made to stand still in some way. Our memory must capture the present before it can be an object of contemplation. Even my knowledge of myself, my sense of self, is formed by such a series of "time-bytes." Somehow or other these speeding bits must be frozen so the mind can turn them over, ruminate about them, and relate them to the rest of reality. The stream of our experiences, our thoughts, our hopes, our fears, are deposited in memory for consideration, and from these we get some idea of the self that contains them. To use Augustine's poetic phrase, passing events leave their footprints in the memory, and through examining these we come to see ourselves and judge ourselves (*The Trinity*, 10.8.11).

This is the reason we must be so careful about our present. What I choose now, the actions I perform now, the fantasies I entertain now, will in some sense be with me forever. I do not have peace with my past and future, which many other animals seem to have. All animals have a sense of the present. They all react to what is happening at the moment. Augustine believed that the higher animals even seem to have memory (*A Literal Commentary on Genesis*, 7.21.29), but it is very different from mine. They may remember the past, but they do not worry or rejoice about it.

Through my powers of sensation I (like my animal friends) can become aware of what is happening in the physical universe around me. But I am different from them in that I am self-consciously aware of the feelings that dash about deep inside: my fears and hopes, my loves and hatreds. Thus my inner self can bring to the perception of the physical world a richness beyond the capabilities of mindless nature. I can compare my present moment to similar experiences in the past and hope or fear that they will be repeated.

Various animals also seem to have some vision of a future (birds fly south and squirrels gather nuts to prepare for coming winter), but there is no indication that they fret or celebrate it. Human beings are the only animals who agonize over a wasted youth or worry about retirement. No dog has ever sent a letter to friends proudly announcing the imminent arrival of a litter.

Only a spiritual being can live in past and future in any real way, and this is both a blessing and a curse. It can be a curse if the past and future imprison me. To live fruitfully in the present (the only time that is real for me) I must let go of the past and avoid living in the future. In order to be "free to be me" here and now, I must not spend all my present moments in reverie about good times past (my "good times" now are in front of me, not behind me) or guilt about my past bad times (they are over and done with and are profitable only in prompting me not to repeat them) or in dreams of "what might have been" (for that is but a fantasy that, given my established limitations, would probably never have been).

In a similar fashion, to be free to be me I must avoid reaching too passionately for the future. To focus on "what is not yet" loses what "is." For a child to spend all its time dreaming about being grown up makes it lose the joy of being a child. Lovers who constantly worry about losing their love in the future will lose the ecstasy of having their love now present. To be constantly depressed by a death that is still to come results in a loss of the delight of being alive.

Augustine believed the only way to have a somewhat happy life here on earth was to deal with our times now, whatever they might be. When we are young we should rejoice in our youth. When we are old we should rejoice in our age. Augustine maintained that every age has its own gifts, and each includes and builds on what went before (*Sermon 216*, 7.7–8.8). Every age—infancy, adolescence, maturity, old age—has its own peculiar beauty, but we cannot enjoy the particular beauty of our present age if we are desperately trying to hold onto the age that went before (*83 Diverse Questions*, 44).

A full human life is like a poem or song where the grandeur of the whole depends on moving from syllable to syllable, from note to note, from age to age (*Confessions*, 11.28.37). Holding onto a past life can be as cacophonous as a song of one note. Living in the future can result in a life as empty as a melody yet to be composed. Being attached to the past can even destroy life. Augustine cites the example of the snake to make this point. The snake must shed the old skin of its youth before it can enjoy the fine new skin of its maturity. To try to stay contained in the cocoon of the past is to jeopardize the future (*Sermon 64*, 6). In a true sense we "make our times" by how we deal with them (*Sermon 80*, 8), and if we are tempted to be nostalgic about days gone by, Augustine reminds us that the "good old days" were not always that good (*Sermon 346c*, 1–2).

Augustine once remarked that at the moment of creation many of God's creatures remained hidden in the "roots of time," developing only long after (*A Literal Commentary on Genesis*, 5.4.11). The same thing (though in a different sense) can be said of each of us. Our roots too are hidden, but not in time. They are hidden in eternity. We were hidden in the eternal knowledge God had of us long before our time came to be. We were hidden in his choice from all eternity to make us in time and to make time for us. Long before time began God decided to place us on the river of time so that we might have a chance to follow the course of its path to the eternal peace that lies just on the other side of the great falls of death.

It is only in the depths of the inner self that we can comprehend this eternal dimension of our lives. It is only in the depths of our inner self that we can respond to those around us with love. Once recognizing the truth of our eternal destiny, we can understand Augustine's advice that we must "redeem our time," that we must stop wasting so much of our precious present on inconsequential conflicts and dissipations, that we must redeem our time by using it to pay for eternity (*Sermon 167*, 3). We can also understand why, at the end of his reflection on time, Augustine prayed:

> Just now my years are consumed by sighs. Time has cut me up into pieces and I do not understand what order is being followed. The deepest places of my heart and soul are being twisted and torn by every kind of upheaval. And so it shall be until that glorious day when I shall be purified and melted by the fire of your love and shall have finally become one with you (*Confessions*, 11.29.39).

On that happy eternal day we can justifiably sing to God that old song (and I hereby hint at how long the stream of my time has run) made famous by the crooner Rudy Vallee in the 1930s:

> My time is your time
>
> and your time is my time.

# The Beauty of the Inner Self

There are some people we *see* with our eyes but we do not really *know* them because we don't know what their internal life is like. There are others whom we have never seen but whom we know profoundly because we know of their love and affection for us. We cannot endure some of those whom we see physically because we do not truly know them. The beauty of their inner self remains hidden until it is revealed by some outward sign (*Letter 205*, no. 1).

Augustine believed that the essential characteristic of beauty is unity. It is for this reason that the absolute unity that is God is the most beautiful of all existing things. Created things cannot replicate that absolute "oneness," but they imitate the divine unity through the order they have among their various parts. All created things are beautiful to the extent that they have parts that are not in conflict. For example, Augustine could become absolutely lyrical in his praise for the beauty of the lowly worm, the brightness of its coloring, the pleasing round shape of its body, the arrangement of its various parts from front to rear organized to preserve its unity. Even the worm (he asserts) has the beauty of due order, even though its beauty is far surpassed by the beauty of the human spirit. No one would like to be an unhappy human, but still no one would prefer being a happy worm as an alternative (*On True Religion*, 41.77).

The difference between the grandeur of the human and the grandeur of the rest of the universe comes down to this: the non-human universe is beautiful because it was made *through* the "likeness" of the beauty that is God; the human spirit is beautiful because it was made *as a reflection of* the "likeness" of God (*Incomplete Commentary on Genesis*, 16.59).

The universe is beautiful not because of the immensity of its spaces and length of its time but because of the order of its inner workings (*On True Religion*, 43.80). So too, in the human being the outer self and inner self have their own proper order and beauty. The beauty of the outer self consists in the symmetry of its parts and in the order of the processes that constitute a person's physical life (*On True Religion*, 40.74). The beauty of the inner self is found in the symmetry between its good choices and the order of reality.

This inner beauty is more remarkable in that it depends on free choice. It is created by a spirit of justice, the ordering of things whereby each is given its proper due (*Commentary on Psalm 44*, 3; *Commentary on Psalm 58*,18). The order of the physical universe depends on the free choice of God making it so; the order of the moral universe depends on the free choice of human beings. The moral order is more fragile because it depends on two creators: God who established its order and human beings who choose to observe it.

The moral order is an order that does not "have to be." When it is preserved by good human choice it is indeed a miracle of freedom and grace, and when humans choose not to observe it the tragic effects are more terrible than any bodily deformity. It is worse to have an ugly soul and a beautiful body than simply to have an ugly body (*On Christian Doctrine*, 4.28.61). The reason is obvious: our inner self (the most important part of our person) is centered in our soul, not in our body.

This fact is brought out by an understanding of what is meant by true love for another human being. Augustine believed that we cannot claim we love another if we are only drawn to them by the beauty of their body. He writes:

> Whoever loves another as himself ought to love that which is the person's real self. But our real self is not our body. Therefore we should not desire or take too seriously a person's body.

> Whoever loves anything in his neighbor other than their real
> self does not love him as himself (*On True Religion*, 46.89).

What is most beautiful and desirable in any human being is
that which is within. The beauty of the body may attract our
attention, but only the beauty of our loved one's inner self can
attract our love (*Commentary on the Gospel of John*, 32.2.1).

The marvelous aspect of such love is that when we are passionate about the beauty of our love's inner self we are enabled
to love them even when they are far away. The inner self is not
confined by space or time because it moves toward its love not
by foot but by affection. As with our love of God, we race toward our human love not by walking or running but by our
craving for them. This is the force that draws us toward them
even when they are far away (*Letter 155*, 13). Physically they
may be at a distance, but the bond of our affection makes us
present to each other. When I stand here and think about my
distant love and reach out to them with my desire, I no longer
*am* where I *was*; in some strange way I am now *with them*. As I
sit here in my solitary space, my spirit flies to them and rests in
their heart (*Commentary on the Gospel of John*, 32.1,1).

Of course, it would be preferable to have my earthly loves
physically present, to be able to embrace them with my arms as
well as my heart. But this is not always possible and sometimes
not appropriate. The body of a loved one may be committed to
another in that total bonding of person to person, which is the
essence of marriage. But hearts may be shared with many. To
love a spouse deeply does not preclude a love of children or parents or a dear friend. There is room in the spirit for many loves
that do not necessarily contradict one another. The beauty of the
inner self may be (and indeed, must be) shared with many if we
are to be true to the divine mandate to love our neighbor as ourselves, a command explained by Augustine as the need to love
everyone as friends or in order that they might become friends.

It is a very good thing that our beauty does not depend on
(though it sometimes may include) the beauty of our outer
self. Physical beauty is dependent to some extent on passing

fashion and taste. My "ugly" may be your "pretty." Whatever our tastes, the "splendor of order" that is bodily beauty is a passing phenomenon in the lives of most of us. Even Augustine (perhaps seeing his aging face in the mirror for the first time) was not immune. He remarks:

> Christ did not promise a long life to us who seem to believe that living a long time is a great thing. He did not promise us that we would live to be old, an age which all desire when it is a possibility but whine about when it is a reality. Certainly he did not promise that our bodies would ever be truly beautiful, a beauty which inevitably is destroyed by disease or very old age. Everyone wishes to be beautiful and to grow old, but the two conditions are opposed to each other. When you are old you will not be beautiful. When old age comes, beauty is long gone. The vigor of beauty and the groaning of old age cannot exist in the same person (*Commentary on the Gospel of John*, 32.9.2).

Augustine clearly believed that (as far as the body is concerned) there is an inherent contradiction between being old and being beautiful (though in my experience there is no similar contradiction between being young and being ugly). But he also believed that if humans make the daily effort to renew their spirits, they will grow old only on the outside. As he wrote to his friend Paulina:

> The inner self is renewed day by day, even though the outer self is falling apart either because of starvation or ill health or an accident or increasing age. This last breakdown from age is inevitable even for those who have enjoyed a lifetime of good health. The solution is to raise up the spirit of that inner self where you will not die when your outer self begins to deteriorate. In your inner self you will not waste away even when your life has become weighed down with years (*Letter 147*, 2).

Inside, the beauty of the spirit remains always young. The inner self can be reborn even as the outer self decays day after day (*On True Religion*, 40.74). Even in our old age we can remain as young in spirit as a child (*Commentary on Psalm 112*, 2).

This does not mean that our outer self should be ignored completely nor that it is wrong to make it presentable. After all, it is as much a part of the person who is "me" as my inner self. There is no harm in dressing it up from time to time. Indeed, Augustine believed that one of the signs of the goodness of the universe is that there are so many things that can make our poor old body healthy and even some that will help make it pretty (*City of God*, 22.24). But there are dangers in cosmetic obsession. As Augustine observed:

> The more attention people pay to the ornaments and frills of the body (the outer self), the more they seem to neglect their inner self. The less concern people have for the trappings of their outer self, the more the inner self is decked out with the splendor of beautiful behavior (*Sermon 161*, 11).

Certainly the value of how we appear is much less than what we are inside, but at the same time our spirit should seek out those things that are good for the body. It should seek nourishment that will make the body healthy and beautiful, assimilating into the body those things that do it good and quickly disposing of any unwelcome and unhealthy residue (*On True Religion*, 40.74). But it would be silly to be more concerned about the passing beauty of our outer self than about the possible eternal beauty of our inner self, to worry more about the shape of our body than the shape of our lives. There is nothing wrong in having a modest posterior, but it is infinitely more important to have a successful anterior, that eternal life that is in front of us. It is important for us to stop looking behind and continue moving ahead by our love for what lies ahead. You cannot keep on walking while examining yourself in a mirror. As Augustine told the people in his church congregation:

> If you are thinking about the things that are to come, forget what is past. Don't look back lest (like Lot's wife) you get stuck there where you turned around. You must be dissatisfied with yourself now if you are ever to make progress. If at any point in your life you become satisfied with what you have accomplished, at that place you will be stuck forever. So always plunge ahead! Keep on walking into your future! (*Sermon 169*, 18).

Perhaps the strongest reason for us to search for our own inner beauty is that if we never grasp its wonder it will be hard for us to begin to love ourselves. It is not too disastrous if, shocked by our reflection in our morning mirror, we declare "I hate my body!" Our disgust may even have a good effect. We may begin an exercise program and diet plan to reshape our crumbling vessel and give it a few more years of vital life. But if we declare "I hate myself" it can be only because we have discovered no beauty, no value, anywhere in our person. We have looked at our inner self and have found nothing to love.

This indeed is a sad state of affairs, because with all our shortcomings there is still much beauty there. We are alive. We still have the power to *know*, the power to wander to places past and future and into lands that can be only imagined. We still have the power to choose, and through that power we have the ability to love. Through that love we can be drawn outside of ourselves to the very heavens. Through that love we can embrace again the memories of all those lovely persons we have met in our lifetime. It is the recognition of this beauty that dwells within that will open us to the world outside, even to the God who is above all. Embracing now our own existence we can approach that one who eternally *is*. As Augustine writes:

> If you more and more have a will *to be*, the closer you will come to him who supremely *is*. Always be grateful that you exist. The more you have loved being alive, the more fully will you thirst for everlasting life (*On Free Choice of the Will*, 3.7).

Put simply, if we find the beauty of our self we have taken the first step in finding and loving God. Only by recognizing the beauty of our inner self can we be led to choose life and look forward with anticipation to a life that goes on forever. In the beauty of our inner selves we will discover the hand of the God who made us to be beautiful, the God who promises us that if we choose life he will ensure that our lives will be eternally bathed in love.

# The Value of My Self

Since we humans in our inner self can achieve wisdom (that is, come to know eternal truths), it is primarily in our inner selves that we are images of God. We, along with many other things, exist and live. But also we can *know,* and in that power of knowledge we are superior to all other created things on earth. Even that outer self that is our body shares some likeness to God in that, through its wonderful powers of sense knowledge, the door is opened to an *understanding* of what this life of ours is all about. True, this old body of ours has no life of its own, but it is still a better image of God than the body of any other animal (*83 Diverse Questions*, 51.2–3).

Despite what Augustine says above, I suspect the sentiment expressed by a friend is shared by many of us, at least on our bad days. She said:

I think the inner self might better be left in the *dark!* It is a kind of wordless history in layers on layers. It's like uncut pages in a book: unread. Sometimes, when material leaks out as it does in a landfill, the stench can be intolerable. It becomes impossible to cover up its effect on us. It seems better to laugh at our all too apparent foolishness and be reassured that below the surface we have those tested "red flags" that warn us of danger without constantly reminding us that we have been hurt before. Perhaps the buried self should remain so. God probably knew that much of what is below the surface is toxic. It remains there to send signals to us which cannot be misunderstood.

Socrates stated: "The unexamined life is not worth living." My friend expresses an equally true principle: "Too much mulling is bad for the soul."

I believe that Augustine would agree with both observations. Diving into our "self" too deeply for too long can make us drown either in our real (or imagined) evil or our real (or pretended) goodness. If I see only good in my inner self, I can be overcome with a pride that will stop me from ever going out of my self. Comfortable in my hubris, I could become so completely at home in the glory of being me that I would see no need or obligation to search for any friend or god beyond myself. I would apply to myself (and only myself) the happy words of Augustine: "God, the wise Creator and just Planner of all natures, has made this fragile race of human beings the loveliest of all the lovely things on earth" (*City of God*, 19.13.2). I would come to believe that not only is the human race the loveliest race on earth, I indeed am the loveliest part of that race. Infected with self-adulation, I would look at my reflection in the mirror and cry out in joy: "Others may be beautiful, but I am BEAUTY!" I would be crazy, to be sure, but I would be at least momentarily happy.

Sadness would come when I look into my self and see only rottenness. Perhaps this is the reason that sometimes we are tempted to end it all. As far as I know, humans are the only animal species that commits suicide. Sometimes we do it because of physical pain, sometimes because of loneliness, sometimes just because we can no longer stand ourselves. At such dark times it is important to realize that, despite all our defects, we are still the most important part of God's creation. As Augustine so powerfully put it, "God has not, does not, or ever will make a *useless* human being" (*Freedom of the Will*, 3.23.66).

Despite all that seems to be wrong with us, we are still "miracle workers," capable of doing great good through our extraordinary powers. Moreover, we ourselves are greater miracles than any miracle we might perform (*City of God*, 10.12). Augustine outlined the wonderful gifts we have in a sermon to the people in his church:

We owe it to God that we are what we are. It is only because of
God that we are *not nothing*. This we share with sticks and
stones, but are we not something more? Indeed, we are *alive*.
But trees and shrubs are alive too. Are we not something more?
Indeed, we have the power of *sensation*. Like the other animals,
we see, we hear, we smell, we taste, and by touch all over the
body we can distinguish soft from hard, rough from smooth,
hot from cold. Do we have something more? Indeed, we have
something animals do not have. We have *mind, reason, and the
power of judgment!* It is through such gifts as these that we can
be truly said to be made to the image of God (*Sermon 43*, 3).

We humans are the best things in creation, and we are all
equal in this noble position. There are no "second class" human
beings, precisely because all humans have the same nature,
which reflects God. We are, indeed, members of one family. As
Augustine says:

What is true beyond doubt for any Christian is the fact that all
existing human beings, however unusual to us may be the shape
of their body, or the color of their skin or the way they walk or
the sound of their voice, however they are endowed or not endowed with natural qualities of strength or ability, all of them
(and ourselves too) are descended from the same human being,
that first human being created by God (*City of God*, 16.8).

Indeed, all of us are members of the one human family,
and God our Father and friend is present *equally* in us all. As
Augustine told his listeners:

The sermon which I am uttering with my tongue, spilling out
sounds broken up into letters and syllables, is heard equally by
all. It is not cut up in different sized pieces to be given to this
one and that one. All possess it equally. So too, the God who is
everywhere is possessed equally by everyone. And so, my
friends, do not be upset by the differences in fortune you see
around you, that some have positions of honor and others have
no honor, that some are rich and others are poor, that some are
beautiful and others are not so beautiful, that some are worn
out by age and some still have the vitality of youth, that some

are men and others are women. God is equally present to all. The one who has more of God in his life is not the one who has more money but the one who has more faith (*Sermon 47,* 30).

In that one human nature shared equally by all, we all have the potentiality to perform extraordinary acts of knowledge and choice. Though many animals can know, only we know that we know. Only we can reflect on the past and laugh about it or grieve over it. It takes a deep appreciation of order to be amused by the sometimes disorder of our past. It takes a deep awareness of the "way things should be" to grieve over a past that sometimes did not live up to that ideal. Only such a mind as ours can go beyond the surface of things and recognize the rules that make things work as they do. Only a human mind can look beyond the present "is" to a future "not yet" and plan to make it better and hope that it will be so.

And more, of all the animals, we have the power to choose our future, to "make" our future. Of course, in this life we do not have absolute control over what will happen to us or what others will do to us, but we always have the power to choose our response to those events. This is one meaning of Augustine's words: "We *are* our times. Let us live well and our times will be good. Such as *we* are, such are our times" (*Sermon 80,* 8). A more important meaning of his words is that what we choose ourselves to be in these times of our lives will determine how we shall be for all eternity. Even if we cannot make our times to be what we would like them to be, we can determine the nature of our eternity, and no one can take this power away from us.

In our infinite thirst to know and in our freedom to choose we best reflect the powers of God. Our glory is that we carry within us the image of the Divine. Our burden is that we carry that precious image in a vessel that is imperfect. We have great gifts and great powers, great hopes and great ideals, but our actions are sputtering. We are engines that are somewhat out of tune. We may not be junk, but we do need repair. We all race through life with a slight limp. But even in our somewhat disabled existence, a life that has bruised us in its passing, we can still enjoy many things that are good. We are alive and still able to make decisions that can create a better future in eternity.

Augustine never gave up on himself and never gave up on any other human being. He firmly believed that "where there is life there is hope" (*Commentary on Psalm 36/2*, 11). Admittedly we sometimes make a mess of our lives and the lives of others, but even so, would it be better for us to have been some lesser creation, a mole digging blindly in the earth, a cup of wine sitting innocently on the table? Augustine's answer is a resounding "No!" It is better for a free being to have lived and lost than never to have lived at all. A free but evil human is still better than an animal that has no choice but to be good, to be what its nature has made it to be. A stray horse is better than a stone that cannot wander, but a freely wandering human is better than a horse that never leaves the barn (*Freedom of the Will*, 3.5.15).

Humans who get drunk on wine are sadly wasting the best that is in them, but they are still better than the wine that makes them drunk. A bad wine is forever bad, but a bad human can change. We still have the power to dream of a better life and to choose it with the help of God. No other beings can do this because no other beings have as much of the Divine within them. All of creation is good, but we are the *best* and have it within our power to act that way. It is for this reason that, however disreputable we may seem to be to ourselves and others, we may always apply to ourselves the sentiments expressed in one of Augustine's letters:

> If the creation of living things should prompt from us the greatest praise of the Creator, how much more should the creation of a human being? The reason why any human is created is simply because God is good. Thus, if you ask why any person exists, the answer is simple: because this person is good (*Letter 166*, 15).

Even in our darkest hour God still says to us, "If you are going to praise the works of God, you should begin with yourself for you too are a work of God" (*Commentary on Psalm 144*, 7).

# The Love of Self

When God gave you the two commandments of love (love God and your neighbor), he did not think it necessary to order you to love yourself. There are no human beings who do not love themselves, but there are many who will lose themselves by loving themselves in the wrong way. When we were told to love God with our whole self, we were given the way we should love ourselves properly. Do you want to love yourself? Love God with your whole self and you will find yourself. If you stay confined in your self, you will lose yourself. If you love only your self, you will fall away from yourself and go wandering among things that are outside your self (*Sermon 179a*, 4).

If we have come at last to value ourselves, to respect the goodness in ourselves, then we are prepared to take the next step: to love ourselves. There is a great difference between admiring and loving. We can admire at a distance; to love means to desire union. With respect to ourselves, there seem to be two ways in which we avoid such union. Of course we always are what we are. We are one, and there can be no separation without destroying our self. But we can distance ourselves from our self psychologically, something like those who claim a near-death experience of floating to the ceiling of their hospital room and from there witnessing the death throes of the suffering self below. We can become so filled with disgust at the evil we find in our inner self that we are simply repelled. Far from loving our self, we hate our self for what we are and have become.

A more common form of separation from self is reveling in a "wrong kind of love," a love that seeks self-satisfaction through every kind of pleasure accomplished by any kind of means. It is a life lived with no guiding principle except the fulfillment of the desire of the moment, ignoring the poisonous effects on others or oneself. Augustine warned his church assembly about such love:

> The real death for any person is from iniquity. Every worldly pleasure is someday going to pass away. As a consequence there is a love that is useful and there is a love that is harmful. People do not have the love that is useful for salvation because they do not want to give up their harmful love. They are filled up with the love of sensual pleasure, love for gold and silver, love for their possessions, love for every good of this present life (*Sermon 368*, 3).

Such selfish love is death-dealing because it rejects the God of life for the pleasures of the present life (*Sermon 368*, 2). It is in fact a hatred of self. The self wants to be served and pleasured by things that are below it while at the same time rejecting the One who is above it. In so doing it fulfills the prophecy of the psalmist: "Whoever loves iniquity hates his own soul" (Ps 11:5) (*On Christian Doctrine*, 1.23.23).

Augustine did not believe it was wrong to seek things below us as consolations on our sometimes tedious trip through time, but our primary love must be love of God (*Sermon 368*, 5). Without some kind of love for God we cannot love ourselves, and if we do not love ourselves we cannot love others. As Augustine says:

> You must *first* learn to love God and *then* you can come to love yourself. After that you can take the next step and begin to love your neighbor. If you can't even love yourself, how will you ever be able to honestly love your neighbor? If by loving your vices you not only *do not* love yourself but in fact *hate* yourself, how in the world can you be able to love God or your neighbor? Therefore, if you wish to observe the true order of charity, begin by acting justly, loving mercy, shunning self-gratification. Try to love others, not only your friends but even your enemies.

If you try with your whole heart and soul to follow these in-
structions, these virtues will be like a flight of steps on which
you can climb towards being *worthy* to love God completely,
with your whole mind and strength. When you reach the rap-
ture of this blissful state, you will realize that all those worldly
goods and pleasures you desired before were but the decaying
rubbish of passing time. Then you will honestly be able to say
with the psalmist, "But for me to cling to God is good" (Ps
73:28) (*Sermon 368*, 5).

Admittedly, the plan outlined by Augustine seems confus-
ing if not circular. It goes something like this:

Step 1: We must love ourselves before we can reach out in love
to others.
Step 2: We must love others before we can "climb the steps" to
perfect love of God.
Step 3: We must love God first if we are to truly love ourselves.

How can it be that we cannot love God unless we love ourselves
and yet we cannot love ourselves if we do not love God? Perhaps the paradox can be explained in the following fashion. It
is indeed true that the process must begin with love of ourselves. But in order to love ourselves properly we must have at
least the *beginning* of a love for God, even if that God is as yet
unknown formally. How do we begin to love a God we do not
know? This beginning of love of God is found in our attempts
to live a moral life in which we "act justly, love mercy, and shun
self-indulgence" (*Sermon 368*, 5).

If we reject any attempt to live a somewhat moral life, we
embrace iniquity and "kill" our soul by eliminating all chance
for eternal happiness. By filling ourselves up with the wrong
kind of love, one that drags us down, there is no room for the
right kind of love, a love that will lift our lives into the heavens
(*Sermon 368*, 3). This is true hatred of self; as virulent as a passion to condemn our enemies to hell. Indeed, it is even more
deadly. Our damnation of our enemies is ineffectual; our destruction of our own chances at salvation is within our control.

Augustine believed that the hatred of self manifested by a "wrong sort of love" (a love of iniquity) was common among human beings, but he does not seem to believe that an *absolute* hatred of self was possible. On this point I must disagree. I believe there is another form of self-hatred characterized by a downright disgust for the filth one finds covering the depths of one's self. Looking inside our conscience and remembering our past depravity, we are horrified. We are unable to stand ourselves. Of course we may still "take care of ourselves" by doing those things demanded for self-preservation. We may even indulge in practices that seem aimed at pleasure, but even these exist in an environment of self-hatred.

Not all drug addicts or drunkards or those satisfying vile perversions think highly of themselves. Indeed, their apparently self-serving lives sometimes mask a deep aversion to self. They have looked into the face of their own depravity, the terrible warts that have disfigured their spirit, and have become indifferent to the damage they do to themselves. They have looked but found nothing in themselves that is admirable, nothing good, nothing worthy of love.

Such lack of love for ourselves can cause a despair that comes from a conviction that my "nothingness," my non-existence, is much to be preferred to my useless continuing existence. Such self-hatred is the worst aspect of the disease of scrupulosity. Infected with this terrible disease of the spirit, it becomes impossible for us to believe that we are free from sin or that we have been honest enough in confessing it. We go again and again to God and repeat again and again the same faults only to leave dissatisfied. We cannot believe that God loves and forgives us because we are unable to forgive and love ourselves.

It stands to reason that this disgust with self would also make it impossible for us to go out to others in love. While respect can be one-sided (I can respect you even though you do not respect me), love by its nature is reciprocal. If I cannot love myself, if I cannot be comfortable with myself, if I cannot even "put up with" myself, it becomes impossible for me to believe I can be loved by others. Despairing of the return of love, I may not even try to declare love for them. I may desire them over a lifetime, but I will smother any thought of being united to them in love, thinking the corruption I perceive within myself would disgust them. After all, a garbage dump has few if any expectations of affection.

If I am convinced that I am buried in the deepest part of the pit of ugliness, I will never reach out in love seeking love from anyone because everyone seems more beautiful than I am (*Commentary on the Epistle of John*, 9.9.1). How can I seek the ecstasy of loving union with someone when the "me" in such union is worth nothing at all, indeed *is* nothing at all? The principle *Bonum diffusivum sibi* (good spreads itself out) applies equally well to love. If there is no love for my self, there is nothing to disperse to others. Clearly this "not loving self" because of disgust with self is more deadly than "loving self wrongly." If I love wrongly by wasting my life in loving the worldly *things* around me, there is at least a *something* there. If I lose myself in excessive affection for a *human love*, there is at least *something* there. But if I cannot love *myself* at all, I am suffocated by *nothingness*; I exist in a vacuum created by my own hopelessness.

The only solution to such abject despair with self comes from a faith that tells me how deeply God is involved in my daily life. Faith tells me that the only reason I as an individual have the ability to love is because God has given me the *power* to love (*Sermon 34*, 2). God has also supplied the highest *object* worthy of my love by revealing God's own self through the incarnation. In the person of Jesus Christ, God shows (though "through a glass darkly") something of the goodness and mercy and gentleness of Divinity. Finally, through the influence of grace God *supports my act of love* by influencing me to love what should be loved, drawing me out of myself by making love of neighbor and God more desirable than staying selfishly involved only in my self, an egocentrism that would cause me to lose myself forever (*Sermon 34*, 7).

We must find some beauty in the self if we are to love it, and beauty is created by love. Augustine was convinced that as hideous as human beings may become because of sin, they should always remember that God has made every person's soul beautiful:

> Our soul is hideous because it is deformed by sin. Only by loving God can it be made beautiful. God is always beautiful, is never misshapen, is never changeable. And he who is always beautiful is the same one who has loved us *first* in our frightful and ugly state. He loved us in order to change us from our hideousness and to make us beautiful (*Commentary on the Epistle of John*, 9.1.1).

It is a strange and wonderful thought: God makes our ugliness to be beautiful. It is not unknown that a beautiful person will love another who is terribly ugly. However, their love does not destroy the ugliness; it overlooks it. In the eyes of our beloved we seem beautiful, but we remain ugly. It is only the love from God washing over us that can take away the corruption, the vileness, the stench that we humans have created in our selves by the evil we do. And that is exactly what Jesus Christ, the Son of God, did through his life and death. He came in his beauty to take up our ugliness and destroy it.

If we cannot love ourselves it is because of our own weakness, our own "cracks." Either we have become so disgusted with our self we cannot see the beauty in ourselves that God created, or we have ignored that interior beauty through our passion for everything except God. We love other things too much and have lost interest in reflecting on what our obsessions have done to ourselves. This is indeed unfortunate, because only when a balanced and appropriate love for self has been accomplished will we be ready to take the next step in our search for and union with God. Before we can escape from self in a productive way, we must love our starting point: the depths of our own self.

# Forgetting the Self

> Just as your self has been fleeing from itself, so too has it been flee-
> ing from its God. It looked at itself and became very pleased with
> itself. It became a lover of its own power. The solution is to love
> God so ardently that, as far as possible, *we forget ourselves* out of
> love for him. We were living a topsy-turvy life when we forgot
> ourselves out of love for the world outside. Now we must forget
> ourselves by loving the Creator of that world (*Sermon 142,* 3).

We make progress toward God by a process of remembering and forgetting. First of all, in order to discover our true
self we must first "forget" external temporal things. Not that we
lose all knowledge of them (after all, we must continue to live
in this world), but we must forget them in the sense that we are
no longer attached to them or consumed by them. Though we
still take care of our bodies, we do not make their care and their
pleasure the end all and be all of our existence. Though still interested in what is going on around us, we no longer spend all
our precious time thinking about or discussing the events and
foibles of the passing world. Though still interested in being a
success in this life, our earthly ambitions take second place to
our desire for eternal success. We no longer sacrifice principle
in order to get ahead; we, following the example of John the
Baptist, hold ourselves ready to lose our head for a noble cause.
It is only by "forgetting" the external world that we come to remember our true selves.

Then we must go beyond our self. This is necessary because perfect happiness cannot be found in our isolated self any

more than in the fleeting goods of the external world. In some way or other, after all our strenuous effort to get in touch with ourselves, we must now forget our selves and move beyond the cramped borders of our own person. We must turn our attention to other persons and to God. It is only by thus forgetting self that we can discover the fullness of self, the self now not isolated in some solitary box but embraced by and embracing divine and human lovers. As Augustine told his friends:

> Christ says to you: "Look me in the face! Are you willing to clutch yourself so tightly that you will lose everything? If you wish to hold onto yourself, you must first hold onto me. To put it another way, you must hate yourself out of love for me. You must preserve your life by sacrificing it for my sake. If you do not, you will lose it by clutching it too tightly" (*Sermon 345*, 2).

The path we must follow to achieve final happiness is a process of discovering and then moving on, a process of "remembering" and then "forgetting." As we have said before, discovery of the external world and becoming aware that it is different from one's self is the way we begin our lives. As young children we spend our time more in seeking food and rest and pleasurable experiences than in self-analysis. Only by eventually "forgetting" the external world do we come to discover ourselves as an object of love. Then, by "forgetting" ourselves we come to discover others as objects of love.

But once we discover the wonder of human love, once we have embraced our human lovers, the process of "forgetting" must begin once again. These human loves (like our own self) may be part of the perfect happiness we seek, but they cannot be its supreme source. They, like the rest of creation, are passing. They are temporal, transient, and imperfect. Our affection for them may last till the end of time, but they will not. Like it or not, there will be a separation, perhaps through death, perhaps by a "going separate ways" in life. Like the great goods of this world, our human loves are not meant to be our final resting place. We must be ready to move beyond them if we are to take that final step in our search: the discovery of and union with God. With our attention no longer preoccupied by our human loves, we are ready to move beyond them to God. Once that discovery takes place (and it will be perfected only after death) then we can return to the world and our self and our human loves more ardently, now seeing them in the various wonderful ways in which they reflect the beauty of God.

This process was outlined by St. Augustine in one of his last conversations with his mother. It was a few days before her sudden death, and mother and son were sitting together in a garden in Ostia, the seaport of Rome. They were waiting for a ship to take them back to North Africa. Augustine describes the scene as follows:

> My mother and I were alone speaking to each other in an intimate and quiet manner. Forgetting what was in the past, we stretched out our attention to what was ahead. We discussed with each other (aided by your enlightening presence, O God) what the eternal life of the saints in heaven might be like. Our reflection brought us to the point where we realized that the pleasures of the body, no matter how intense and brilliant they might be, would be unworthy of comparison and even remembrance when the joys of heavenly life were experienced.
>
> Our longing lifted us up ever more passionately towards the God who is "That Which Is." Step by step our desire drew us beyond all earthly creatures and then beyond the heavens above where the sun and moon and stars bathed the earth in light. Our awed reflection and wondering dialogue about your great works eventually brought us to the very summit of our own minds. Then we went even beyond this and touched that land where you feed Israel (your chosen ones) with the food of truth. There is the place of God, that "Wisdom" which is the source of all that is created, that Wisdom that has no "has been" nor "will be" but only an eternal "I Am."
>
> And suddenly, as I and my mother talked and longed for this land, we touched the edge of it by an awesome leap of our hearts. Then we said to each other:

If the bedlam of the flesh fell silent in a person's life, and silent too were all earthy experiences, if the sea and the air and the heavens themselves should suddenly become filled with silence, and if the human spirit itself became quiet and was able to pass beyond itself by *not thinking* about itself and, in a flash of intuition, touch that Eternal Wisdom that dwells above all things . . . if this experience could last forever, would this not be indeed the joy of the Lord? (*Confessions* 9.10.23–25).

For a moment mother and son had "forgotten" the world around them and the world that was their self. Empty of all this, they were able briefly to achieve a preview of heaven. For a moment they "experienced" the presence of God (*Confessions*, 9.10.24).

The ecstasy of mother and son ended there. In less than a week Monica would be dead. In less than a year Augustine would return to Africa, there to spend the last forty years of his life. As far as we know he never had an experience of Divinity again, but the memory of that day at Ostia lingered on. The process of reaching God by forgetting the world and by eventually even forgetting the self became central to his teaching ever after.

# Escaping Self

> When you leave God out of your life and love only yourself you
> flee from yourself. You begin to cherish things outside yourself
> more than yourself. You must, therefore, first come back to
> yourself. Then, when you have done this, you must direct your
> love towards others. It would be a mistake to stay trapped in-
> side your own self. True, you must come back to your self from
> your attachment to the *things* outside, but then you must es-
> cape yourself by giving yourself back to God who made you
> (*Sermon 330*, 3).

Forgetting self establishes the condition for moving further
in our search for perfect happiness, but the force that will actually
move us is our love for those beyond ourselves. To be trapped in
exclusive love for self leads to stagnation. To have forgetfulness of
self without movement toward others leads to oblivion. We lose
both ourselves and the rest of reality. There is no progress in ad-
diction to self. We cannot increase or grow if our desire feeds
upon itself. Love can only move my self further when its object is
beyond my self. When our passion for self remains contained
within, we literally begin to eat ourselves alive, cut off from all external nourishment, becoming dead and barren.

This is what happened in the story of Narcissus from
Greek mythology. He was frozen in place by the ecstasy caused
by seeing his own beautiful face. He became so enchanted by
his own reflection in the still waters of a pond that he could not
tear himself away. He died alone on the shore, not because he
did not love, but because he could not get beyond his love for
himself. He learned the hard lesson that we cannot become

whole if our love stays directed only at ourselves. If all we care about is our life, our success, our leisure, we become like Narcissus—a lump on the shore. Narcissus could not develop the sacrificial love that is the only way humans can get beyond themselves to reach the kingdom of God.

It is a strange but true fact: we can only make ourselves holy by emptying ourselves of ourselves, escaping ourselves and reaching for that one good that will perfect us, the good that is God. Augustine expressed this truth in the advice he gave to his friends in a sermon. He told them:

> Don't stay trapped inside yourself. Rise above yourself and place yourself in the hands of the God who made you. I am not saying that you must destroy yourself. And yet, on the other hand, I have the audacity to tell you that you indeed must die to self. This is necessary because if you have died with Christ, then you will seek only those heavenly goods that are far above yourself (*Sermon 153*, no. 9).

No doubt the people in Augustine's audience were upset when they heard his words. Even the phrase "sacrificial love" can be frightening when you first hear it. You think of the bloody tearing apart of a helpless animal on an altar of sacrifice. You think of Abraham ready to plunge his knife into the heart of his beloved son Isaac. Is this the love we are called to practice as human beings? Are we supposed to destroy ourselves for the sake of God?

In a way we are. Christ has told us that we must love as he has loved, and Paul tells us that Christ loved us with a love that emptied him out. He emptied himself of his own self so that he could fill himself with our humanity, so that he could experience our weakness, so that he could take to himself our malice and sinfulness in order that he might save us and make us sacred. That is precisely what sacrificial love is meant to do. It is a love that makes sacred. It is the love to which God calls us so that we can become his sacred, holy place finally and forever.

The paradox is that the principal place of God in creation is deep within each one of us (*Sermon 53*, 15), and in order to find God we must go inside the depths of our self. We obviously cannot discover God if we rush outside our self through our love for the things of this world. But also we cannot discover God inside or outside our selves if we become so fascinated with our self that we move no further. As Augustine says: "If you selfishly and solely love yourself, you will lose yourself. Once you fall away from the God who dwells within, you lose your very self" (*Sermon 179a*, 4).

When we free ourselves from the things of self, those consuming loves for things and pleasures and success, then we leave room in ourselves for the love and presence of God. And when our love reaches out from our emptiness toward God, we cannot stay empty very long. God rushes in to take up residence in a new and special way. This is what the great martyrs did. They died to themselves and thereby came to God (*Sermon 159*, 8).

But how can we develop such love? We do not see God. We cannot really "do" anything for God. Is it just a matter of proclaiming our love and leaving it at that? Augustine points out that love is exercised not by words but by deeds, and true love of the God we do not see must begin through love for each other. He says:

> You say to me "I have not seen God." Well, can you say to me, "I have not seen human beings"? Love your fellow humans. If you love those whom you can see, then you eventually will see God (*Commentary on the Letter of John*, 5.7).

Augustine only repeats the message of the New Testament when he says, "If we have love for each other, we thereby exhibit a true love for Christ" (*Sermon 229n*, 1). This is so because Christ is in our neighbor just as he is in us. It therefore follows that when we love other human beings, living in their hearts through our love, we also begin to dwell in Christ and he begins to dwell in us. Our hearts dwell in the objects of our love (*Commentary on the Gospel of John*, 2.11.2).

This sacrificial love, which expresses itself in good works for those around us, now becomes true to its name. We have emptied ourselves of self by reaching out with our affection, our gifts, our concern, our very self, and in the vacuum that results there is now a place for God. God floods our life and makes our "self" a sacred place. In some mystical sense we have *become* sacred. It is hard to fathom how this can happen, how indeed we can become *like God*. It was equally hard for Augustine. But he did believe it and preached it to his people, telling them:

> Do you love God? What shall I say? That you will be God yourself? I don't dare to say such things on my own, but listen to what the psalmist (speaking in the person of God) says: "I have said 'All of you are gods and children of the most high'" (Ps 82:6). It follows then that one who does the will of God abides forever in a god-like state just as God also abides forever (*Commentary on the Letter of John*, 2.14.5).

In loving other human beings, in being concerned for their welfare, in trying to help them, we are loving Christ and making room in the temple of our self for the coming of the Lord. His presence will never be perfect in us during this life, but if he has at least a foothold, a little bit of space in our lives, to that extent our love will have made us sacred. And with God in us that love can energize us and push us along the road home to that place where we shall completely be in God and God in us.

That is what God wants above all. The grand mystery of human life is that, though we were created as finite human beings with a hunger for happiness, we cannot achieve happiness unless we become like gods, becoming that sacred place created by our sacrificial love. This is the place where God dwells in time. It is the place where we will eventually come to enjoy God forever in eternity.

How we reach that place through love of others and love of God is a complex topic, and its discussion must be reserved for another time and another place. But if we have discovered our true self and are prepared to move on, we will have accomplished the first part of Augustine's prayer "Oh unchanging God, let me know myself; let me know you" (*Soliloquies*, 2.1.1) and will be well on the way to accomplishing the second.